FIRE UPON THE EARTH

ABOUT THE AUTHOR

The Reverend Canon J. E. Fison is the author,
among other books, of *The Blessing of the Holy
Spirit* (Longmans, 1950) and the 'Pelican' book
entitled *The Faith of the Bible*. His interest in
biblical study was quickened by his acquain-
tance with the contemporary life of the Jewish
and Arab communities when he taught in a
Mission School in the Middle East and served
as an Army chaplain in Egypt and Palestine.

FIRE UPON THE EARTH

by

J. E. FISON

" I came to cast fire upon the earth ;
And how I wish that it was now kindled ! "

(LUKE 12 : 49 : T. W. Manson)

LONDON
EDINBURGH HOUSE PRESS
2 EATON GATE, S.W.1

First published 1958

CONTENTS

I wish to thank my wife for reading the entire manuscript and for making many often resisted but nearly always necessary corrections of its mistakes and clarifications of its obscurities. The book has had other " helps " (1 Corinthians 12 : 28), but none to equal this.

J. E. F.

MAKE ME THY FUEL

From prayer that asks that I may be
Sheltered from winds that beat on Thee,
From fearing when I should aspire,
From faltering when I should climb higher,
From silken self, O Captain, free
Thy soldier who would follow Thee.

From subtle love of softening things,
From easy choices, weakenings,
(Not thus are spirits fortified,
Not this way went the Crucified)
From all that dims Thy Calvary,
O Lamb of God, deliver me.

Give me the love that leads the way,
The faith that nothing can dismay,
The hope no disappointments tire,
The passion that will burn like fire,
Let me not sink to be a clod:
Make me Thy fuel, Flame of God.

AMY CARMICHAEL

NOTES

S. (=Saint) is only used of the writers of the four Gospels and their works. No theory of authorship (or canonization !) is implied.

Bible references are to the Revised Version unless otherwise stated.

Permission from the Dohnavur Fellowship for the inclusion of the poem *Make Me Thy Fuel*, by Amy Carmichael, is gratefully acknowledged.

PREFACE

IF the Holy Spirit is God " intimately present and active within ",[1] then there is the greatest need for him to be allowed to be " intimately present and active within " every individual Christian soul and the Christian community as a whole. We are therefore presented with two problems. The first is : how can the Spirit be given such unhindered right of way ? And the second is : if he is given such unhindered right of way, how can we be sure that he is the Holy Spirit, and not another counterfeit ?

To these two questions, it is possible that the following survey of the biblical evidence may provide most interesting and, indeed, exciting answers. For the Old Testament can be interpreted as showing, first, the need for the Spirit's unhindered right of way in and through the unconscious and subconscious depths of the individual soul, so closely linked with the group as a whole. That is the work of the primitive Spirit (ch. 1). Then, working in and through the individual and often in the teeth of community opposition, comes the challenge of the prophetic Spirit (ch. 2) to man's conscious will : parallel with this is the appeal of the priestly Spirit (ch. 3) to his emotions and feelings ; and then, finally, the stimulus of the philosophical Spirit (ch. 4) to his intellect. Thus all aspects of life (goodness, beauty and truth ; morality, art and science) are integrated in the kingdom of God.

When we turn from the Old Testament to the New, we see the unhindered operation of the pietist Spirit (ch. 5) in an intimate circle of friends, the expanding range of the Pentecostal Spirit (ch. 6) in the growth of the universal Christian church, and the unlimited scope of

[1] H. H. Farmer, *Revelation and Religion* (Nisbet, 1954), p. 79

the Pauline Spirit (ch. 7) in the whole of man's individual and corporate life. Thus, successively, are revealed
seven stages, or facets, of the Spirit's work.[1] In the end
he has unhindered right of way both in the individual
soul and in the life of the community as a whole.

But how can we be sure that this Spirit is Holy ? The
question does not arise until the unfettered action of
God " intimately present " has been secured and demonstrated " within " the individual and the community.
But when it has been so secured and demonstrated, the
question forces itself urgently upon us, and the answer
to it in the Bible is the Johannine doctrine of the Paraclete
(ch. 8). It is the work of the Spirit who is Holy always
to point to Jesus Christ, so that thus Jesus Christ may
live afresh in every age in the lives of those who are
baptized into his death and live in holy communion
with him. " He shall baptize you with the Holy Ghost
and with fire." [2]

---

[1] But all sub-divisions of the ways of the working of the " one and the
self-same Spirit " are arbitrary and abstract ; even if in analysis they can
be separated, in life they always co-exist and overlap.

[2] Matthew 3 : 11

CHAPTER I

THE FIRE OF REVIVAL AND THE PRIMITIVE SPIRIT

THERE is something odd and uncanny and (by our standards) utterly abnormal about the outbreaks of *ruach*, or Spirit, in Judges [1] and 1 Samuel,[2] and it may well be that it was their very oddity and abnormality which caused these strange phenomena to be attributed to *ruach*—the inexplicable wind which blows up so suddenly from the desert and dies away again so mysteriously. Like the desert wind, that comes up suddenly from nowhere, so this uprush of the unconscious, this possession by the subliminal, this overwhelming of normal conscious behaviour seems to come from nowhere —or at least from somewhere very much below the level of consciousness. It seems to be a reaction to the primitive, a throw-back to the elemental, and a breaking down of all man's carefully built-up protective walls of conscious convention and habit.

This is a biblical fact to be taken with all seriousness and not to be belittled on the ground that we are more civilized than the ancient Israelites and that our ethical standards and æsthetic tastes are better than theirs. Of course, this uprush of the primitive, the elemental and the unconscious, this ' possession ' by the Spirit, is not the be-all and end-all of the biblical evidence for the doctrine of the Holy Spirit. But it is the starting point of that doctrine, and only if we are prepared to start where the Bible starts are we likely to know in experience anything of the higher reaches of the Spirit's work. We cannot jump the queue.

[1] Judges 3 : 10 ; 6 : 34 ; 11 : 29 ; 13 : 25 ; 14 : 6 ; 15 : 14
[2] 1 Samuel 10 : 6 ff. ; 11 : 6 ; 16 : 13

If Judges and 1 Samuel are written off by some Christians as ethically sub-standard, the story of Pentecost [1] cannot possibly be so dismissed. The evidence of Acts 2 is backed up by almost every other reference to the Holy Spirit in the Acts of the Apostles [2] ; the hallmark of the Spirit's work is not immediately recognizable in ethical conduct or spiritual insight, but rather in strange, odd and otherwise unaccountable behaviour. This often seems to take the form of the liberation of previously inhibited elements in the subconscious or unconscious.

The tapping of these elemental energies and the releasing of these vast subliminal fires of explosive power are fraught with immense danger. But these things are the secrets of everything creative within us. Contact between the Infinite and the finite, the Holy and the sinful, the Creator and the creature, can hardly fail to be explosive in the nature of the case, and the biblical evidence makes plain the often quite devastating character of the explosion. There can be no knowledge in experience of the Holy Spirit without a willingness to expose to him the unplumbed depths of the subconscious and unconscious. The risk of a relapse to the primitive and elemental crudities of the past has got to be taken, if the chance of pushing on towards the creative possibilities of the future is to be seized. Either the " great deep " [3] must be " broken up ", or there can be no creative power.

And where is this " great deep " likely to be found ? The outbursts of *ruach* in Judges and 1 Samuel are almost entirely connected with the rise of Israelite nationalism and the struggle for independence and freedom from foreign oppression. While we are not obliged to accept every crude interpretation of the Spirit's work, we shall

[1] Acts 2 : 1 ff.
[2] Acts 8 : 18 ; 10 : 19, 44 ; 15 : 8 ; 19 : 6
[3] cf. Genesis 7 : 11

do well to pause before we lightly dismiss this remarkable connection. For, in the first place, the biblical evidence puts the outburst of the Spirit on the Day of Pentecost in a strikingly similar context ; and, in the second place, it is precisely such a torrential outburst of the primitive and the unconscious, connected with nationalism, which threatens to overwhelm our modern world.

Let us examine the biblical evidence more closely. The struggle for independence under the banner of nationalism is self-evident in Judges and 1 Samuel. But have we ever stopped to think what was the peculiarity of this nationalism that made it different from all other Middle Eastern nationalisms of the ancient or the modern world ? Perhaps, in our heart of hearts, we do not think it was different, and so write it off as a primitive element in our inherited religious tradition, which we can now quite properly discard. Nothing, I venture to think, would in our modern world be more improper, if we have any inkling of the true character of our religion or any desire that it should continue in the world as a living force and not merely as a dead fossil.

Israel's nationalism was unique, and its uniqueness lay in the uniqueness of Israel's " jealous " nationalist God, Yahweh. The other gods of the Middle East were Baals. They belonged to the soil, and the soil belonged to them. They expected, and they usually got, blind, unthinking allegiance from those who lived on the soil and whose lives depended on it. Baal and his worshippers were bound together by nature, not by choice : so much was this so, that the end of the nation or tribe which lived on the soil meant the end of the Baal too. Although, therefore, the word, Baal, indicates a male divinity (who often had a consort, Astarte), the kind of worship and devotion offered to Baal was the kind of worship and devotion offered to Artemis or " Diana of the Ephesians ",[1] or to Cybele, the Great Mother of Asia Minor.

The nature of the difference between the religion of Baal and Diana of the Ephesians on the one hand and the religion of Yahweh on the other can be illustrated from a very common psychological phenomenon of our time. In an age when so many parents are seemingly indifferent to their children and so many children apparently could not care less about their parents, there is evidence all around us of the devastating effect of possessive parents (usually mothers) upon their children.

The mother perhaps quite unconsciously exercises such a controlling grip upon her child that the boy or girl, tied to mother's apron strings, never really grows up to have a mind and will and character of his or her own. Such mother-possession is far too common in our modern Western world with its small families, and its attempt to prevent the break-up of the home is a most potent cause of that break-up.

In the face of the twin perils of mother-indifference and mother-possession, our age needs nothing so much as a true sense of mother-security, which gives children the confidence that they are always wanted, valued and loved, regardless of sins, mistakes and failures, and so enables them to make a constructive contribution to the life of the world in which they live. The creative fire of genuine personal enthusiasm springs out of the freedom of mother-security ; the ultimately destructive fire of impersonal fanaticism derives from the bondage of mother-possession ; and the lack of all enthusiasm or fanaticism is the tragic consequence of indifference to mother.

The relationship between Baal and his worshippers was a relationship of mother-possession, which could produce a fanatical enthusiasm of the most destructive kind. But over against this mother-possession, or

[1] Acts 19 : 28

motherland-possession, of the typical Middle Eastern nationalism stood the religion of Yahweh, which was the dynamic behind Israelite nationalism. This also offered security, but the security of grace, not merely of nature ; the security of free choice as well as heredity. Yahweh's religion begins with an exodus, a coming out of the womb of mother-possession, not in order to live without any real mother-relationship at all, but in order to make the truly creative adventures of life, which spring from a genuine sense of mother-security.

Although Judaism always professed to worship Yahweh, it was always—and not merely before the Exile—in danger of worshipping him as a Baal, of however improved or refined a variety. This led to its false attitude of mother-possession, and it was precisely because of this false attitude that Jesus found he could only do his Father's will by breaking not only his mother's heart [1] but also the heart of his mother-land and his mother-church. Baptism involved just this same agonizing break for the early Christians. It presupposed an intense nationalism, and it involved a breaking out of that nationalism into the true mother-security offered by the Christian church, which replaced the false mother-possession claimed by the Jewish church.

The intense nationalism of the Jews in the time of Jesus Christ is often written off by Christians as something entirely negative and as an obstacle to the coming of the kingdom of God, because it obviously had so much to do with the crucifixion of Jesus and the rejection of his Messianic claims. We need to ask whether such a verdict is justifiable. The last question put by the apostles to Jesus before his ascension was a nationalist question : " Lord, dost thou at this time restore the kingdom to Israel ? " [2] This question invited rebuke, and it got it—but how gently Jesus administered the rebuke and how insensibly he switched this nationalist

[1] cf. Luke 2 : 48   [2] Acts 1 : 6

aspiration onto the international vision of Pentecost and all its world-wide possibilities ! " It is not for you to know times or seasons, which the Father hath set within his own authority. But ye shall receive power, when the Holy Ghost is come upon you : and ye shall be my witnesses both in Jerusalem, and in all Judæa and Samaria, and unto the uttermost part of the earth." [1]

The world-wide international mission of the Christian church is entirely misunderstood unless it is seen as a break-out of an intense Jewish nationalism. It is doubtful if those who have never felt the emotional pull of such mother-possession, or been swept off their feet by the appeal of some other primitive or subconscious urge, can have any knowledge of what the Old Testament means by the two words, which it hardly ever uses together, ' holy ' and ' spirit '. And only those who have made the heart-breaking cut of this tie of mother-possession can fully understand what the New Testament means by putting them together as ' Holy Spirit '.

Their meaning is first ecstatic and apparently irrational and, if you like, mystical. It is only afterwards moral and ethical. So the primitive Spirit is primarily manifested in things that are odd, abnormal and uncanny. These things happened in the Old Testament, and they happened in the New. They are still happening today, but how seldom in the ' great church ', which is usually more than content to keep a respectable distance from them !

It may be difficult in a traditional Western Christian church today to let ourselves be carried away by enthusiasm and run the risk of being thought drunk at 9 a.m.[2] It was no easier in the traditional Middle Eastern Jewish church on the Day of Pentecost. As soon as its implications were realized, it meant then

---

[1] Acts 1 : 7 f.

[2] Acts 2 : 15—drunk at 9 a.m.—and the only evidence that it is not due to alcohol, the fact that it is 9 a.m. !

complete separation and ostracism—socially, politically, economically and religiously—from the community to which you belonged. There is no reason why it should not mean the same today. The fire of revival depends on the primitive Spirit : we can have it, if we are willing to pay the price for it, but the price will not come down. Calvary precedes Pentecost.

* * * * *

In the light of the biblical evidence, where are we likely to find the fire of revival " upon the earth " today ? " Our God is a consuming fire " [1] sounds more like Zeta and nuclear energy than a cathedral service or a prayer meeting ! In view of the close connection in the Old Testament between the fire of the primitive Spirit and the rise of Jewish nationalism, and in view of the experiment in communism in the New Testament immediately after Pentecost, the obvious place to begin our search is in the contemporary nationalist and communist movements in the world today. We should not be deceived about the deep similarity between the two, however great the superficial difference between a local nationalist and a universal communist Baal.

The fires of nationalism and communism are sweeping Africa and Asia today, and the fierce flames of racialism are blazing, not only in South Africa, but in Arkansas as well. There is fire in the fanatical supporters of *apartheid* as well as in the defence of the Johannesburg treason trial. The deepest tragedy of Africa is that the fire which we hate with a fiery hatred may be the very fire of which we are most in need. [2]

The fact that it can lead us to destruction and eventually land us in the mass hysteria and fanatical grip of a Nuremburg Nazi rally, or the disgusting obscenities of a Mau Mau ritual, should not blind us to the peril of so

[1] Hebrews 12 : 29
[2] cf. L. van der Post, *The Dark Eye in Africa* (Hogarth Press, 1955)

avoiding the demonic fire that we never touch the divine. Lives lived in a mediocrity of boredom are no more likely to reflect the glory of the Creator's aim for all who are made in his image than voyages in which men and women venture to set their sails to the winds of the primitive Spirit and are swept away over the uncharted seas of the unconscious.

What we see in the worst excesses of racialism, nationalism and communism, as well as in the finest fruits of patriotism, we can see in music and art as well. There is fire in the primitive urge that sends European painters out to the South Pacific, and D. H. Lawrence and Mexican painters back to the ancient Aztecs, and which sends sculptors to Benin in West Africa, and musicians to the Negro spiritual and its ancestral roots, in search of some new inspiration. We can catch a glimpse through the Tartar dances of the Russian Bolshoi ballet and through the classic style of Ulanova of the overwhelming effect of the primitive Spirit, when tremendous elemental vitality finds expression in perfect form.

From nationalism and art it is not a far cry to religion. We can see the fire today in the Pentecostal sects, the Billy Graham crusades, M.R.A., the great Roman Catholic eucharistic congresses and the German Protestant *Kirchentag*, and certainly at Lourdes in this centenary year, 1958. And who would deny the renewed fire of the ancient faiths of Asia, as well as the pure flame of the Revival Movement of Kenya in the midst of the foul fire of Mau Mau?

Nothing is as futile as the condemnation by respectable established churches of the excesses of revivalist, prophetic and Pentecostal sects. It is the fire the latter so manifestly exhibit that the former so woefully lack. A church merely conducted " decently and in order ",[1] in

---

[1] 1 Corinthians 14 : 40. The apostolic exhortation was as relevant in the first century Corinthian church as it is manifestly irrelevant in so many British churches today.

the face of the challenge of communism, nationalism and rock 'n roll, has no gospel for today. There is no possibility of contact with the divine without running the risk of being destroyed by the demonic. That is why biblical religion at its best is the deadly enemy of the false " safety, certainty and enjoyment " of mother-possession. It is always either bliss or perdition, salvation or damnation, the greatest curse or the most wonderful blessing in life. It cannot be the one, without running the risk of the other : promise and peril must always co-exist.

So long as we refuse that total commitment to the Creator by the creature, that humbling awareness of the Infinite by the finite, and that hazardous encounter between the Holy and the sinful, which are only possible when the great deeps of the unconscious as well as the shallows of consciousness are broken up—for just so long we shall have no reality in our conscious experience to correspond with the words, Holy Spirit. We may say with truth that we have received the Holy Spirit because God has promised to give him—both in the church in baptism and confirmation and outside it apart from any rite or ceremony " to them that ask him ".[1] But what is the value of a cheque for one thousand pounds, if we do not cash it ? If the Bible did not contain the promises, and if the church had not given the guarantees, what in our own experience, individually or corporately, has ever been or is now so odd, so peculiar, so extraordinary that, to describe it, we should have to coin a new word and then find to our surprise that we could not improve upon the ancient definition—Holy Spirit ?

If we want to enter into the true meaning of this reality, perhaps an illustration from the theatre may give us a clue as to how we can do it, for this universe is the theatre which exhibits the drama of creation, and

[1] Luke 11 : 13

our earth is the stage of the drama of redemption also. If we are not willing to ' let ourselves go ' and be carried away by the drama on the stage, we cannot hope even to understand it, let alone take any part in it. Of course, after we have been carried away, we must ' come to ', and think with all the earnestness at our command about what we have seen. But first things first—and it is not conscious thought, or our search for God, but willingness to be swept away by our unconscious or subconscious reactions to the drama of his search for us, which is the pre-condition of all that follows.

I had the chance last year of a talk with a spiritualist, who speaks every Sunday, and often on weekdays, too, without (so he told me) ever consciously knowing what he says. Such unconscious ' automation ' is not the hall-mark of the full and final revelation of the Holy Spirit, and if it should lead away from or be in any way a denial of Jesus Christ, I should regard it as something much more like demonic than divine possession : but by comparison with the few, who today confine the Holy Spirit to the level of the unconscious, how many limit his work to the level of consciousness—and at that level, in consequence, know nothing of it !

We have not all got to become automatic spiritualists or violent nationalists before we can become true Christians. But we must be prepared at some time or another —the sooner the better, but better late than never !—to be swept off our feet by some great cause or ideal to which we give ourselves wholeheartedly. To stay in our depth at such a time may be to escape the demonic : it is certain to miss the divine. This is the meaning of Christian baptism, and it has been a fatal consequence of transferring *en bloc* the full doctrine of adult baptism to infant baptism that the false idea has grown up that the Spirit could be fully given, even if the great deeps were not broken up.

It is true that the Spirit must move first : the initiative

is always God's. But so far as our conscious experience goes, it is certain that baptism into Christ's death, with all that that means of being both lost and saved in the depths of our soul, is the pre-condition of being filled with the Holy Spirit. That is why the early Christians limited the work of the Spirit to mother-church. They did not deny the work of God outside the church, but they knew from experience that the fire of the primitive Spirit was to be found inside the church in a way it could not be found outside. It could not burn in souls that were not in relationship with their mother. If that relationship was mother-possession, as it was with Paul, in devoted bondage to his mother Jewish church before his conversion, it needed converting into true mother-security, which is what Paul found after his conversion and baptism in the Christian church.

Without any relationship with mother there can be no fire. Out of the false relationship of mother-possession the fire breaks out in destruction. Out of the true relationship of mother-security comes all the fire of creative energy. It is useless for Europe and America to deplore the destruction of so much of the nationalist and communist fire now sweeping across Asia and Africa. The tragedy of Europe and America is the absence of any fire. The only answer to the false fire is the true : the only answer to mother-possession is mother-security.

Where can we see signs of the true fire of the primitive Spirit in the church today ? There is certainly fire in the prophetic and Pentecostal sects, though the fact that it is religious and not political should not prevent us from seeing that, like nationalism, it may just as well be the fanaticism born of mother-possession as the genuine enthusiasm springing out of mother-security. Close to the Pentecostal sects in some respects, but very different from them in others, the Revival Movement [1] of the East

[1] cf. M. A. C. Warren, *Revival: an Enquiry* (S.C.M. Press, 1954)

African church may prove to be the most significant sign of the working of the primitive Spirit in the world today. If anything is able to provide a basis of unity for the multi-racial society of Kenya, it may turn out to be no grandiose political scheme, but this humble movement, springing from the primitive Spirit.

There is fire, too, in some of the courageous attempts to make the church truly indigenous in countries where it has for too long worn a foreign aspect. Coming to terms with legitimate nationalist aspirations, whether at the high level of a Vatican concordat or at the low level of trying not to offend in matters of clothes and architecture, may be nothing more than Christian self-interest in survival. But it may have within it a true dynamic of the Spirit. If the Reformation shows the dangers, it also shows the possibilities of such a connection between religion and nationalism. The Reformation doctrine, that a man's religion depends upon the region where he lives, looks quite as much like mother-possession by a local Baal as the Roman Catholic excesses of devotion to the Blessed Virgin Mary look like mother-possession by a universal Baal. But without the Blessed Virgin Mary, the alternatives seem to be the secularist pin-up or the Puritan denial of sex, and without some connection with nationalism, how can any religion ever become indigenous anywhere?

To be able to worship God in a light which shines through Egyptian windows, as in the Gairdner Memorial Church of Jesus, the Light of the World, in Old Cairo, or through Nigerian windows, as in the unfinished Cathedral of the Holy Spirit at Onitsha, is a sign of the times. The primitive Spirit may here be harnessing true patriotism to the service of the universal church, though there is a danger that in the younger churches of the twentieth century, as in the older churches of the Reformation, the elemental fire may prove more destructive of the past than creative of the future.

There is fire, too, in some of the attempts to re-capture the vision of earlier ' ages of faith'. This may be nothing more than a flight to antiquity, but if it is a withdrawal into the past in order to return to face the present, with the elemental energy of yesterday thereby put at the disposal of today, then such a withdrawal may be a real means of rekindling the primitive fire. The flame of the primitive Spirit is certainly burning brightly in the Protestant monastic communities, of men at Taizé in France (so thrillingly near to the scene of the great mediæval monastic reform at Cluny), and of women at Grandchamp, near Neuchatel, in Switzerland.

In the same way, the revived interest in Gregorian plainsong, associated especially with the abbey of Solesmes, may be based upon a similar hunger for the primitive Spirit. Is it too much to hope that, if only this ancient tradition could be cross-fertilized by the elemental inspiration of the Negro spiritual, an entirely new liberation of the Spirit might occur ? Father Geoffrey Beaumont's Folk Mass shows which way the wind of the Spirit is blowing, and the conversion of the Salvation Army brass band at Leicester into a skiffle group may be more than a straw in that same wind.

It is not easy to fit the enthusiasm of biblical funda-mentalism, Dr Billy Graham's evangelistic crusades, M.R.A., Roman Catholic eucharistic congresses and the German Protestant *Kirchentag* into any true pattern of the spread of the fire of revival today. The primitive Spirit that is imprisoned in a bondage of mother-possession is very close to the primitive Spirit that is liberated by the inspiration of mother-security. But one thing is certain : a church which is merely bourgeois and middle-class, a church which is primarily ethical and intellectual in its interest, a church which speaks only to man's conscious-ness—however clear its gospel message—such a church has no answer to the deepest needs of our time. These are elemental, and not superficial; and any internationalism, which ignores this fact, or any œcumenicalism, which imagines it has got beyond it, is spiritually bankrupt to meet the challenge of 1958.

CHAPTER II

THE FIRE OF THE WORD AND THE PROPHETIC SPIRIT

IT is one thing to recognize and tap the primitive and elemental energies of the unconscious : it is quite another thing to see that the energy so tapped is directed aright. If the great deeps are touched and their power liberated, everything depends on the purpose for which that power is used and the object towards which it is directed. The elemental outbursts of Judges and 1 Samuel, and even sometimes those of Acts, are not immediately or necessarily directed towards ethical ends. And in both the Old and the New Testament we are confronted by strange and significant silences.

The great prophets of the Old Testament are very sparing in their references to the Spirit. They attribute their inspiration to the word, *dabar*, of the Lord, rather than to his Spirit, or *ruach*. Furthermore, Amos' explosive rebuttal of any possible allegation that he belonged to the discredited prophetic profession is couched in much stronger terms than his testimony to the continuity of genuine prophetic revelation.[1] Not only are the prophets after Amos chary of claiming the inspiration of the Spirit ; they are also very reticent about calling themselves prophets at all.[2]

The simplest explanation of this silence is that the prophets in the Old Testament, just like Jesus in the New, want to dissociate themselves from the strange abnormalities of the ' spirit-possessed '. They want to reclaim consciousness for God, and are unwilling to limit the activity of his Spirit to the subliminal and the unconscious. They are conscious of what they say and

[1] Amos 7 : 14 and 3 : 7   [2] Hosea 9 : 7

15

are fully responsible for their words. These words are intelligible to those to whom they are spoken and they are intended to produce a conscious response. The fire is being controlled for creative and constructive ends : the question is, to what ends ?

If the Spirit spoke through the prophets, what exactly did he say through them ? Or, to use their own language, what was " the word of the Lord " which they spoke ? Why did they speak it ? And to whom did they speak it ? The prophetic tradition stems in continuously revived succession from Moses. No one after Moses was ever quite Moses' equal : the Old Testament tradition is perfectly clear about this.[1] Nevertheless, it is as a prophet and as the head of a great succession of prophets that Moses stands forth against Pharaoh and, in Professor Buber's great phrase, confronts the rule of royalty with the rule of *ruach*, or Spirit. " By a prophet the Lord brought Israel up out of Egypt, and by a prophet was he preserved." [2]

This tradition of Protestant opposition to potential or actual tyranny remains a permanent part of the prophetic witness. Moses confronts Pharaoh, Nathan confronts David ; Elijah confronts Ahab, and Micaiah the son of Imlah confronts Ahab and Jehoshaphat. In addition, Ahijah the Shilonite intervenes against the tyranny of the Solomonic dynasty on behalf of Jeroboam the son of Nebat.

All this adds up to very substantial evidence that one of the main ways in which the Spirit spoke through the prophets was in violent protest against any attempt by any man to usurp to himself arrogant and absolute power

---

[1] " The Lord spake unto Moses face to face, as a man speaketh unto his friend " (Exodus 33 : 11). " If there be a prophet among you, I the Lord will make myself known unto him in a vision, I will speak with him in a dream. My servant Moses is not so ; he is faithful in all mine house : with him will I speak mouth to mouth, even manifestly, and not in dark speeches ; and the form of the Lord shall he behold " (Numbers 12 : 6 ff.)

[2] Hosea 12 : 13

over other people's property or persons. Nathan challenged David on a personal matter—the seduction of Bathsheba and the death of Uriah. Ahijah instigated a rebellion against the Davidic monarch—a protest, perhaps, from old Shiloh and its shrine, against the new use of the Jerusalem Temple as an appendage to the royal court. Elijah challenged Ahab's right (at Jezebel's instigation) to take over Naboth's vineyard, and Micaiah opposed a military expedition.

These brave and courageous interventions by a succession of prophets were never on behalf of any general ethical principles : they were always related to particular wrongs, and opposed definite sins, and therefore in form they were largely negative, even if cumulatively they add up to an impressive testimony on behalf of the ethical character of the God in whose name they were made. But there is more to even early Hebrew prophecy than just this negative opposition to sin : the prophets are at the very heart of the national resistance movement. It is impossible to deny the inspiration of Deborah the prophetess behind the most significant outburst of patriotic fervour in the pre-monarchical period, or the direct responsibility of Samuel the prophet for the creation of the Israelite monarchy. But the story of the choice of Saul and his early career suggests that Samuel's original support for the monarchy was later qualified by his increasing awareness of Saul's limitations and, indeed, of his disqualifications for his exalted position. Such disillusionment was the lot of many prophets.

Isaiah's early enthusiasm for Hezekiah was not entirely vindicated by the king's later career, and his confidence in the inviolability of Zion was directly challenged by Jeremiah's doctrine of appeasement one hundred years later. Jeremiah's own early confidence in the Temple reforms of King Josiah was bitterly disappointed in the sequel. Deutero-Isaiah's early hopes of Cyrus were only partially fulfilled, and in consequence his Messianic vision altered its focus from the great Persian Emperor to the greater Suffering Servant. And so it went on : from Haggai's hopes of Zerubbabel to the tremendous enthusiasm for the early Maccabees, the story is one long record of expectation, partial fulfilment, and then final frustration and disappointment.

This is a fact of the greatest importance for a right attitude to prophecy and for a true understanding of how God once spoke and still speaks through prophets. When a prophet speaks the word of the Lord, it is not to utter generalized statements of universal truth, capable of particular application in given concrete situations. On the contrary, he speaks directly to the present concrete situation, and about this situation he speaks a definite and decisive word. This word is usually unconditional in form—it is categorical, not hypothetical—but it depends for its efficacy and application, upon the co-operation or non-co-operation of those to whom it is addressed.

The story of Jonah makes this point abundantly clear. In form, Jonah's message is one of unconditional doom upon Nineveh. There is no qualification whatever about the terms of his pronouncement : " Yet forty days, and Nineveh shall be overthrown ".[1] But in fact, much to Jonah's own chagrin and annoyance, Nineveh repented : " and God repented of the evil, which he said he would do unto them ; and he did it not ".[2]

The Spirit, therefore, speaks through the prophets, not in general pronouncements about universal truths, but in particular denunciations of quite specific sins and in concrete application of particular truths. The prophet's words are often reinforced by symbols, which are not to be regarded as extraneous proofs of the authenticity of his message, but as visible embodiments of it. In some mysterious way it is through the symbol that the thing

[1] Jonah 3 : 4 [2] Jonah 3 : 10

begins to come to pass, no matter whether it is Isaiah
" walking naked and barefoot ",[1] or Ezekiel acting a sort
of dumb charade with a tile and a pan,[2] or even Hosea
marrying a harlot.[3]

Willingness to stake all on a correct interpretation of
a current event is of the very essence of prophecy.   This
is what it means to walk by faith rather than by sight, or
statistics !   The latter are not to be despised, but their
importance is not to be exaggerated, as if it was the
political wisdom and acumen of the prophets which
enabled them to divine the moment both for the call of
Saul and also for his rejection, for the denunciation of
Israel and Judah and for the calling in of Assyria, " the
rod of mine anger ",[4] for the fearful message of the
futility of Jerusalem's resistance to Babylon and for the
glorious hope of Cyrus' edict of toleration, with the
opportunities it gave the exiles to return to the Holy
Land.

The prophets were not political fools : they had their
wits about them, and in this they contrasted sharply with
the frenzied ecstatics of Judges and 1 Samuel.   But
because they had their wits about them, they did not
cease to behave in queer, ecstatic and eccentric ways.
So much is this the case that Ezekiel, the father of almost
everything creative in post-exilic Judaism, and one of the
greatest of the Old Testament prophets, exhibits behaviour which would now be regarded as decidedly
abnormal, if not definitely pathological.

In the prophets the Spirit speaks, or the word of the
Lord comes, through consciousness as well as the unconscious.   In the words of Paul, " the spirits of the prophets
are subject to the prophets ".[5]   But this does not mean
that conscious reflection on political or social or international events is the secret and source of their inspiration.

---

[1] Isaiah 20 : 2   [2] Ezekiel 4 : 1ff .
[3] Hosea 1 : 2   [4] Isaiah 10 : 5
[5] 1 Corinthians 14 : 32

That inspiration may well, being supra-rational, only come to human consciousness via the sub-rational.[1] It is from his awareness of God and his sensitiveness to God's mind and will rather than from his awareness of contemporary world events and his sensitiveness to their significance that the prophet derives the secret of his utterance.

It is in the coincidence of event and interpretation that revelation so often consists. Miriam the prophetess interpreted the significance of the event of the crossing of the Red Sea,[2] and this revelatory conjunction of event and interpretation is emphasized in the Hebrew scriptures by the grouping together under the general heading, *The Prophets*, of the books that we should naturally divide into two distinct classes, prophetic and historical.

We have already noted the absolute form of the prophetic word and remarked that this may conceal its conditional character. But not all non-fulfilment of biblical prophecy can rightly be explained on these lines. It seems to be of the essence of genuine prophecy that if the prophet is ever to be right at the right time— and not just ' after the event '—he must always run the risk of being wrong, and in fact often is wrong. To wait for fool-proof certainty of being right is to walk by sight and not by faith.

Except on a dictaphonic and automatic and sub-human conception of the mode and manner of divine inspiration, there is no guarantee whatever that prophets are always right. On the contrary, the biblical prophets were often wrong and often made mistakes. It is one thing for us to see hidden meanings in scripture : it is quite another thing to claim that these are the original sense of the prophets' words. We do the prophets as grave a disservice by trying to save their ' face ' and

---

[1] " It is through the sub-rational that the supra-rational is brought to human consciousness " (V. White, *God and the Unconscious*, Harvill Press, 1952)   [2] Exodus 15 : 21

pretending they were always right, as we do the saints by trying to save their ' face ' and pretending they were always good.

Two further things need to be said about the way the Spirit spoke through the prophets. First, he did not give detailed information about the future, from which his hearers or readers could deduce the appropriate practical action in the present. On the contrary, he gave practical and pointed comment on the present, from which general principles of how things would work out, or God would act, in the future, could be deduced. This is not to deny an element of prediction in prophecy : it is to set it in its right perspective. When later apocalyptic with its visions of the future lost touch with its prophetic roots in the present (from which it is a legitimate growth), it lost touch with the real world and deserted it for the world of phantasy and make-believe, and escapist and compensatory wishful thinking.

Secondly, the Spirit spoke through the prophets about the situations in which the prophets found themselves. Of course, the horizon of the prophets was often far wider than that of other contemporary Israelites. Amos sensed the threat of Assyrian invasion long before anyone else had an inkling of it. Judgment on the little nations surrounding Israel was part and parcel of his prophecy, just as judgment on the great empires of the Middle East was part and parcel of the greater prophecies that followed his. But all Amos' judgments upon Israel's neighbours were only stepping stones, leading up to his judgment upon Israel herself.[1]

True prophecy is never theoretical : it is always ' existential '. The prophets stand up against the sins of their own people : they do not deal with the sins of others, except in so far as such an extension of the scope of their prophecy follows inevitably from its own fundamental premises and doctrines. It is true that Amos was

[1] Amos 1 : 3–2 : 5, and 2 : 6 ff.

a southerner from Judah and prophesied in the northern kingdom of Israel. For this very reason, perhaps his external diagnosis needed supplementing by Hosea's subsequent internal healing remedies. But this is a very slight exception to the general rule, for Amos lived at Tekoa, which is not much more than twenty miles from the chapel royal at Bethel where he preached. And as an exception, it only proves the general rule that the prophets spoke not only to their own day but also to their own people. They were implicated up to the hilt in their prophecies.

If prophets are ever in short supply, it is not because of any lack of them. Amos' words are always true : " Surely the Lord God will do nothing, but he revealeth his secret unto his servants the prophets ".[1] No : there are plenty of prophets ; the trouble is that either they dare not speak to the people, or they are not allowed to.

*   *   *   *   *

If there is " fire upon the earth " today, is it prophetic as well as primitive ? Can we see any signs of the sort of thing happening that the prophet Jeremiah describes ? " I will make my words in thy mouth fire, and this people wood, and it shall devour them "[2] : " Is not my word like a fire ? saith the Lord ; and like a hammer that breaketh the rock in pieces ? "[3] This is strong language, and it describes the tremendous effect of the prophet's words and the actions with which he incarnated and symbolized their meaning. Are there any such prophetic ' signs of the times ' today in the form either of judgments upon contemporary sins or of pioneering ventures and creative experiments ?

If we look first at Europe, a prophetic Spirit certainly inspired the resistance of both the Confessional church and the Roman Catholic church in Germany to the diabolical excesses of Nazism. It is only necessary to

[1] Amos 3 : 7   [2] Jeremiah 5 : 14   [3] Jeremiah 23 : 29

mention the names of Karl Barth, Martin Niemöller and Cardinal Faulhaber to prove the point. This courageous witness was continued during the war by men like Dietrich von Bonhoffer and the Roman Catholic Archbishop of Munster. After the war it took the moving form of a confession of guilt by the leaders of the German Evangelical Church, at Stuttgart in October 1945. This might have opened a new era of spiritual achievement if it had been more readily followed up, and more generously welcomed and responded to.

In the U.S.A. and Africa the same strong prophetic protest against tyranny has been heard in a very different way from the Negro leaders in the United States, like the Rev. Luther King of Montgomery, Alabama, and from Dr Alan Paton, Father Trevor Huddleston and the Rev. Michael Scott on behalf of the Bantu peoples of South Africa. And, most significant of all, there has been the heroic stand against the excesses of Mau Mau of the Kikuyu members of the Revival Movement, under the inspiration of Obadiah Kariuki, now Assistant Bishop of Mombasa. Here is a glorious example of the genuine prophetic expression of the primitive elemental Spirit.

In Asia there have been the stupendous achievements of Mahatma Gandhi and also the land reforms of his successor and true prophet, Vinoba Bhave. It is probably true that the upsurge of nationalism in both Asia and Africa has been accompanied by genuine prophetic fire and enthusiasm in more cases than we realize. Such a Spirit certainly inspired some of the original members of the group of young officers who overthrew the government of King Farouk in Egypt, and it looks as if the present leadership of South Viet Nam may have a similar motive. It was the prophetic Spirit which inspired Toyohiko Kagawa in Japan in his social experiments before the war, and it is the same Spirit which is now inspiring the social efforts of Abbé Pierre in Paris.

But perhaps the most striking illustrations of the prophetic Spirit in the contemporary Christian church are to be seen where, in experiments such as Dr George McLeod's Iona Community and the Protestant monastic ventures at Taizé and Grandchamp, the inspiration of the primitive Spirit is harnessed to a positive purpose. These are creative modern responses to that challenge to rediscover the meaning of community which has been responsible for so much of the success of world-wide communism.

Whether Karl Marx would himself have been a true prophet—and a Hebrew prophet at that—if he and his family had had a different Christian church experience after their conversion from Judaism, must always remain one of the insoluble ifs of history. But it would be churlish to deny something of true prophetic zeal and enthusiasm in such communist or near-communist community experiments as have been one of the most significant features of the rise to independence of the modern Israeli state. Even if the revolutionary prophetic communism of the early church of Jerusalem has much less in common with contemporary communism than most Marxists like to admit, it is much closer to it than many Christians are willing to allow. And the heroic ventures of the original French priest-workmen under the inspiration of Cardinal Suhard may well have been suppressed after the great cardinal's death because of the ecclesiastical authorities' fear of communist contamination.

This French experiment, born in part of the close collaboration of Catholics and communists in the resistance movement during the war, had a true prophetic stamp. So also had Archbishop William Temple's social achievements, which culminated in the Malvern Conference of 1941. And as for Bishop R. O. Hall's ordination of a Chinese deaconess to the priesthood at Hong Kong under stress of quite exceptional circumstances, this may have been considered wrong by the

Lambeth Conference of 1948, but far better false experiments than no experiments at all ! Would that there was more evidence for such ventures in the Christian church today !

Modern artists, musicians, and poets may not often be prophets, but who would deny the right to something of that title to people like Eric Gill, C. S. Lewis, Dorothy Sayers, and Albert Schweitzer, even more perhaps for his interpretation of Bach than for his work at Lambaréné ? Nor may we exclude from our survey such descendants of Jules Verne as the modern writers of space fiction, for, where their deep prophetic roots are not cut, apocalyptic visions of the future can stake an undoubted biblical claim to be expressions of the prophetic Spirit.

When anyone like David Low, the British cartoonist, or Diego Rivera the Mexican painter, or even Picasso, is speaking in any way on a burning contemporary issue, it is possible that he may be a prophet. If he is speaking at great personal sacrifice to himself, it is more than possible that he may be a true prophet. The prophetic Spirit always presupposes the primitive, and it is so often the artist or the poet who gives expression to the primitive. There can be no word of the Lord or utterance of the Spirit relevant to our present situation, without recognition of the fundamental fact that the unconscious, as well as consciousness, is involved in genuine prophecy. The prophet must risk being wrong if he is ever to be right in time. The multiplication of reports and surveys of all sorts, invaluable in their rightful secondary and subordinate place, makes it very easy for the prophet to be stifled by the statistician. And the appalling consequences of his errors, which will be magnified one hundredfold by modern methods of publicity and propaganda, make it exceedingly hard for the prophet ever to speak the truth in time for it to be of saving and life-giving significance. Either he will not speak at all, or he will speak too late, or he will claim infallibility for his utterances—either on biblical or ecclesiastical or experiential grounds—in order to save himself from the agony of soul through which alone the Spirit can ever speak a truly prophetic word.

A further difficulty is caused today by the prophet's own conscious awareness of so much that happens, that is no direct prophetic concern of his. Owing to modern means of communication, he can so easily put the world right in general theory as an escape from putting right in practice the particular wrong with which he is inescapably confronted in the circumstances of his own life and home situation. We can ban the H-bomb in a resolution and yet be quite unconcerned at the sort of training our young national service men may be receiving. We can speak about dictatorships abroad and yet keep silent about dictatorial relations in trade unions and industry in our own country. We can attack *apartheid* in South Africa and yet ignore the coloured population in our own city and refuse to face the question of mixed marriages between the races, the fear of which bedevils the whole subject. We can speak out—and often "unadvisedly, lightly and wantonly"—about pagan idolatry and witchcraft, of which we probably know nothing at first hand at all, and yet keep a discreet silence about the spurious substitutes for real religion which abound in our own country. Especially where our families are involved—and when their social, educational and financial security seems threatened—we are fearful of speaking up on any relevant and contemporary issue.

But that is what the prophets always do. They are not afraid to speak on contemporary events, whether in nature—e.g. an earthquake or a drought—or in international affairs—e.g. the rise of Cyrus—or in social behaviour—e.g. the luxury, male effeminacy and female masculinity at Samaria—or in the most intimate details of personal conduct and behaviour. And if there is one characteristic of the biblical prophets which stands out above the others, then it is the inflexible standard of righteousness, without a trace of self-interested favouritism anywhere, which marks their interpretation of the will of God for the world in which they lived.

Would all this suggest for our own contemporary scene an end to vague generalizations and a resolute refusal to speak of the evils and injustices of other countries, communions and classes unless or until we are sure we are resolutely and fearlessly facing our own? If judgment must " begin at the house of God ",[1] it should not end there, but only those who themselves sit under judgment are in any position to pass judgment upon others. We must beware of speaking about the sins of others when we are blind to or silent about our own. We must also beware of imagining that generalized church utterances are any substitute for particular prophetic words and deeds.

The prophets were individuals, and the decisions of church councils or committees are no substitute for the prior decisions and utterances of individual prophets. In fact, the decisions of church councils and committees are only likely to have any creative spiritual significance if they are based upon and provoked or inspired by prior prophetic words or deeds. This is strikingly emphasized in the first Council of Jerusalem, for which the guidance of the Holy Spirit is explicitly claimed.[2] The decisions of this council were a compromise—perhaps all such decisions inevitably are—but they were creative, because behind them lay the prophetic individual acts and deeds of the breaking down of the " middle wall of partition " between Jews and Gentiles.

If Peter and Paul, who were individuals, had not ventured to obey the Spirit's leading beforehand, there would have been no point in calling the Jerusalem

[1] 1 Peter 4 : 17   [2] Acts 15 : 28

Council, and certainly no corporate decision it made would have had creative significance for the church. It is because individuals today, out of fear of wrong and irresponsible individual action, refuse to follow the Spirit's leading until they have behind them some council's or committee's decision, or some other form of fool-proof authority, that the work of the Holy Spirit is grievously frustrated and the work of the church's councils and committees themselves is so often sterile. The collective wisdom of the group may be vital to secure a balanced perspective on the many-sided wisdom of God. But—and it is a vital but—the biblical evidence is crystal clear : the prophet precedes the committee and church council, the apostle precedes the apologist. Each is salutary in his rightful place, but each is damnable out of it.

Of course, the prophet may be wrong. There are always false prophets. But our contemporary problem in the established and historic churches is not at all the curbing of false prophets, but the liberation of the true Spirit of prophecy, so that all the elemental energy of the unconscious may be brought into conscious obedience to the will of God and directed towards the diagnosing and healing of the profound spiritual sicknesses of our time. It may not be correct to interpret the destruction of Sodom and Gomorrah as being a direct consequence of the sin of sodomy, as if those sodomites were exceptional sinners above all others. But an incorrect prophetic attempt to relate the two events—the undoubted sodomy and the undoubted destruction—is preferable to the modern habit of refusing to make any connection between them.

There is one incident in the life of Jesus which is of the greatest importance in this connection. "There were," says S. Luke,[1] " some present at that very season which told him of the Galileans, whose blood Pilate had

[1] Luke 13 : 1–5

mingled with their sacrifices. And he answered and said unto them, Think ye that these Galileans were sinners above all the Galileans, because they have suffered these things ? I tell you, Nay : but, except ye repent, ye shall all in like manner perish. Or those eighteen, upon whom the tower in Siloam fell, and killed them, think ye that they were offenders above all the men that dwell in Jerusalem ? I tell you, Nay : but, except ye repent, ye shall all likewise perish."

If our forefathers were apt to be far too glib with their interpretations of historical events, whether of inter-national or of individual significance, we in our genera-tion are so afraid of giving a wrong interpretation or of seeing a false connection, that we often fail to suggest any interpretation or connection at all. Even worse, we have so reduced the living God to the status of a departmental idol, and limited his concern entirely to human affairs, that if we still allow him any connection with morality or church ritual, we have long ago excluded meteorology and earthquakes from his care. If, however, the primi-tive explosions of the Spirit show God's reign in and through the unconscious, then the prophetic expressions of the Spirit claim the whole world of personal con-sciousness, corporate community and cosmic space as the sphere of the operation of the one sole power in the universe.

The prophet knows what is going on behind the scene. If he is to speak the word of the Lord, when that word is relevant to those he is addressing, he will never be able to offer contemporary proof that he is right. But how can the politician act rightly if no prophet gives a lead ? That we have need of prophets to judge us and to comfort us in the modern welfare state is made abundantly clear by the distinction, drawn so sharply in the Wolfenden Report on prostitution and homosexuality, between the sphere of crime, which the law of the state can deal with, and the sphere of sin, which needs the

prophetic voice of the Spirit of God through man, if it is
to be dealt with at all. And if the prophetic Spirit is
needed to rebuke vice, he is also needed to encourage
virtue and, above all, those creative enterprises of hazard
and adventure, which are essential to the continued well-
being not only of the church, but of humanity itself. If
I mention a few such instances of prophetic achievements that appeal to me, I do so not to impose my own
private judgment on others but to invite their private
judgment on many other issues of our time.

First, I believe that Dick Sheppard spoke prophetically
to the world of the 1920s not so much by his pacifism
(though who would deny to the passionate protest of
pacifists like Dr Donald Soper, Dr George McLeod and
Canon Charles Raven a lively prophetic quality?) as
by his readiness to address the people in an idiom the
people could understand. With Dick Sheppard's
introduction of broadcasting into St Martin-in-the-
Fields, the prophetic work of Studdert-Kennedy seems
to me to have come to fruition. Whether Dr Billy
Graham's achievements after the second world war can
be classed with what these men achieved after the first
world war seems at present to be not clear. There are
those who exploit Graham, as Sheppard could never have
been exploited, in the interests of a reactionary and
bigoted interpretation of the Christian faith. But even
so, his work will stand comparison at so many points
with that of John the Baptist that it seems impossible to
acclaim the latter as a prophet without also acclaiming
the former.

Secondly, in the political field we cannot exclude from
the true prophetic role either the work and words of
Mr (now Sir) Winston Churchill in his refusal to sur-
render during the darkest days of the last war, or the
equally courageous decision by Mr (now Lord) Attlee to
quit India by a fixed date, implemented as that was by
the daring heroism of the last viceroy and his wife.

Here are two modern instances (as I judge) of the totally different attitude demanded by the same prophetic Spirit, such as in the great prophets of the Bible is illustrated by the resistance of Isaiah to Sennacherib and the doctrine of appeasement proclaimed by Jeremiah in the face of Nebuchadnezzar's attack in exactly the same place one hundred years later.

Thirdly, turning to theology, for me the poetic, prophetic and philosophical Spirit all uniquely combine in our modern world in the little book of Professor Martin Buber, *I and Thou*. Here is something which touches the philosophical world of the existentialists, is deeply rooted in the biblical world of the patriarchs [1] and the prophets, and is profoundly coloured by the simple piety of Hassidic mysticism ; the influence of those few pages on modern thought has been profound and far-reaching. There have been other prophetic thinkers of our day, and notably the great scientists and psychologists, but none has had such a profound theological influence as Buber ; and Gentile Christians should be the more truly thankful to him, because sometimes in the heated political passions of modern Palestine he seems to have been a prophet ' without honour in his own country '.

Fourthly, if at no point is the prophetic message more needed today than on the question of the colour bar, then I can only draw attention to the possibly supremely prophetic ventures of such intermarriages as are exemplified in the case both of Sir Stafford Cripps' daughter and also of Seretse Khama. Certainly the final success of the missionary work of the church (on the earthly plane) must involve the end both of the white race and of the black. Those who do not want a mixed race should not support the missionary cause.

Finally, if the barrier between colours and races is the deepest problem of our time, there are also other lesser barriers which hinder world fellowship. If these are

[1] cf. M. Buber, *Mamre* (Melbourne University Press and O.U.P., 1946)

allowed to remain, then it seems more than likely that
for this reason alone the cause of communism will
triumph on the stage of contemporary history, because it
appears to offer a solution to the fundamental problem
of the world's disunity. Possibly the last stage of division
between colours, classes and cultures after the levelling
of communism will turn out to be worse than the first
stage of division before the revolution. But future
problematics cannot obscure present facts. And some of
these must be altered, and altered now. It is the belief
that communism will effect such an alteration that gives
it a powerful pull upon the minds not only of the common
people but also of many of the intelligentsia of the
world.

The union of the Atlantic alliance and the British
Commonwealth is vital. But no less vital is the union of
Western Europe and Great Britain. (What a tragedy if
Arab Moslem union precedes European Christian union !)
But where are our Christian prophets speaking out on
behalf of such a union ? Some speak about South Africa
and the colour bar—all honour to them !—but who
speaks about the union of Great Britain and Italy, or of
the United Kingdom and Eire ? What prominent
Protestant or Anglican has faced the problem of what it
will be like to be a minority church in a predominantly
Roman Catholic country ? What hope is there of the
politicians advancing rightly towards such a union, if
the prophets say nothing ?

Yet Christian prophetic speech on Western European
political union could only at this moment invite scathing
criticism of Western European religious disunity. Far
more vital than the Atlantic alliance or the union of
Western Europe is the reunion of Christendom. For
only " in Christ "—and that means in the one reunited
Christian church—can we hope for union across the
greatest modern divison of all, between black and white.
Advances are being made towards reunion ; and it is the

prophetic Spirit who is inspiring them, if they spring genuinely out of the elemental stirrings of the primitive Spirit.

We can truly thank God for the World Council of Churches, but only if it recognizes gladly and unreservedly the contributions of less developed intellects and less informed minds towards its own eventual success. Any tendency by the World Council of Churches to despise the Pentecostal sects, or M.R.A., or the fundamentalist *internationale* (which will have nothing to do with it), or the strong residual nationalisms of some churches, which ignore it, or the depth of primitive religion, still so clearly evident in the Orthodox and Roman Catholic communions, is bound to prove suicidal. If the prophetic outlook does not spring out of the primitive, it has no power to translate into effect the visions which it proclaims to be true.

But if it springs out of the primitive, then it will have to run the risk of being carried away by the unconscious or subconscious, and of being proved wrong to the mature ethical judgment of the church. It is unwillingness to run this risk far more than irresponsible rushing into danger which jeopardizes the future of the Œcumenical Movement. With what joy I went to a church outside Cincinnati in the United States two years ago, which is jointly Episcopalian and Presbyterian ! The courageous action of the Bishop of Southern Ohio in sanctioning such an experiment at an earlier stage of negotiations for closer union between the two churches in the U.S.A. may have been proved unwise. But how much better to make such an experiment, even if it proves wrong—I am in no position to say whether or not it has in fact been proved wrong—than to make no experiment at all !

It is almost inconceivable that a church council will ever make creative ventures towards unity, unless (like the Council of Jerusalem in Acts 15) it meets in order to deal with the situation caused by previous prophetic action. It is for the council to decide whether the action previously taken or the word previously spoken was the action or word of a true or false prophet. But the prophet must speak and act first, and the council must meet afterwards. We do not suffer from a lack of council meetings today—on the contrary we have a surfeit of them—but we suffer terribly from a lack of responsible prophets courageous enough to speak and act in time to affect and influence the contemporary situation.

CHAPTER III

THE FIRE OF THE ALTAR AND THE PRIESTLY SPIRIT

FOR all their greatness, the prophets were men like other men : and for all their unique contribution to the deepening of our understanding of the nature of God and of the terms upon which human beings can live in communion with him, it is quite plain from the biblical evidence that they were not the only medium through which God made his will known to men, nor were they the only channel through whom men could approach God. Advances in scholarship are nearly always marked by inevitably exaggerated swings of the pendulum. Just as a convert tends to exaggerate the contrast between his new life and his old, so biblical scholarship in its first emancipation from the shackles of an infallible book tended to exaggerate the differences and contradictions to be found within the Bible.

One form of this exaggeration was the invention of a complete divorce between the religion of the prophets and the religion of the priests. Sanction for such divorce was found in the categorical denunciations of the sacrificial system found in Amos 5 : 25, Hosea 6 : 6, Micah 6 : 6 ff., Isaiah 1 : 10 ff., Jeremiah 7 : 22 f. These texts were isolated from their contexts and read as the utterances, not of prophets speaking to particular concrete situations, but of systematic theologians enunciating dogmatically for all time a series of sweeping generalizations.

It is now generally agreed by competent scholars that there was never any such absolute divorce between prophet and priest.[1] Isaiah probably had his great

---

[1] Indeed the pendulum has swung the other way. Prophets and priests are almost identified, and ' cultic ' prophets are all the rage !

inaugural vision of God in the Temple itself.[1] Jeremiah came of a priestly family at Anathoth, outside Jerusalem, and almost certainly was heart and soul behind Josiah's Temple reform in 621 B.C. He may afterwards have been disappointed at the comparative failure of the reform, but that does not alter the fact of his initial support of it. As for the third of the great writing prophets, Ezekiel is as much a priest as he is a prophet.

So after seeing what the prophets have to say, we must look now at the priests and see what the Spirit has to say to us through them. References to the Spirit are even more scanty in the priestly than in the prophetic literature. But if we have allowed the claim of the prophets to the inspiration of the Spirit when they speak the word, the *dabar*, of the Lord, there is no reason why we should reject the claim of the priests to a similar inspiration, when they open the way for the communication of the same word by the whole system of institutional religion which they administer. If false prophets do not invalidate true prophecy—and we must remember that the false prophets have always far outnumbered the true —why should a false priestcraft, blocking the way to God by its ecclesiastical paraphernalia and red tape, invalidate the true role of the priest ?

The structure of the Jerusalem Temple was a blueprint, illustrating architecturally exactly what a priest could do. Just as the prophet could speak the word of God, so the priest could open the way to that hidden word, or meaning, or *logos*, which lies behind the surface of everything and alone makes sense of the otherwise incomprehensible variety of human experience and overwhelming complexity of human knowledge. The whole sacrificial system was designed to lead up to and open the way into this hinterland, the Holy of Holies, which was called the oracle, or the *debir*, the place where the " stones of testimony " (the ten Commandments) were

[1] Isaiah 6

originally kept, the place where God's word, or *dabar*, could be heard.

Entrance into this Holy of Holies symbolized that perilous [1] immediacy of contact with the divine and the holy in inner experience, which is the very heart of what we mean when we speak of God as Spirit. God " intimately present and active within ", to use Professor H. H. Farmer's definition, is not an ' adjectival ' extra to, but a ' substantival ' element in all true religion.[2] Without something like this to balance the prophets' insistence on the need to encounter God, the tremendous reality of the latter experience will soon degenerate from living communion into conscious reflection or meditation upon that communion, in which we may get to know much about God, but do not in fact know him at all.

If we allow the Spirit's work in enabling prophets to speak the word of God, we must also allow the Spirit's work in enabling priests to open the way for that word to be heard and understood within the soul. If there were priests who blocked rather than opened the way to God, there were prophets who did the same. And the false prophets as well as the bad priests are with us still ! References to the Spirit in the priestly writings are few, but they are none the less significant. The claim that Bezalel,[3] the craftsman of the tabernacle, was endued with a more or less permanent gift of the Spirit for his particular work certainly shows the atmosphere which pervaded post-exilic worship at its best, even though the prophets had by then been downgraded [4] to a position of inferiority to the priests.

Jewish religion at its best realized that priests and

---

[1] The only person who went into the Holy of Holies was the high priest, and he only went in once every year, on the Day of Atonement.

[2] cf. H. H. Farmer, *Revelation and Religion*, loc. cit.

[3] Exodus 31 : 2 f.

[4] The proof of this downgrading is in 2 Chronicles 34 : 30, where " Levites " replaces the parallel " prophets " in 2 Kings 23 : 2. Pre-exilic prophets = post-exilic Temple singers !

prophets were both needed. The direct word of the prophets was required in order to bring man's will into conscious obedience to the will of God, and thus balance the opening up of the unconscious depths of the soul, illustrated in the psychological abnormalities of Judges and 1 Samuel. The whole sacrificial system of the priests was needed, too, even if its meaning was not fully understood, in order to grip man's emotions and feelings. Thus through prophet and priest the worshipper's whole personality might be caught up into vital communion with the living God. What the word did directly for man's conscious intellect and will, the symbol and the sacrament and the sacrifice did indirectly—by suggestion, rather than dictation—for his subconscious emotions and feelings.

So the Spirit spoke—(a) through the abnormal, primitive and unconscious, (b) through the clear ethical challenge to the conscious will, and (c) through the deep suggestiveness of the sacrificial system—to the emotions and feelings not only of the individual personality but also of the community as a whole. In case anyone should imagine that the work of the prophets and the priests meant any outgrowing of the primitive ecstasy of Judges and 1 Samuel, it is important to remember that even the greatest prophets in the Old Testament were rapt in ecstasy and behaved in fantastically weird and apparently crazy ways, and that the apostle to the Gentiles himself in the New Testament spoke with tongues and was " caught up even to the third heaven ".[1] The uncanny with its wonder remains, no matter how great our advances in knowledge. It is only the atheist who ceases to wonder, and it is only the superstitious man who provides an explanation of the wonder which exhausts its meaning. The genuine man of faith abides in his wonder and all increases of his knowledge of how the wonder works only make him marvel the more at the fact that it works.

[1] 2 Corinthians 12 : 2

It was to make life in this ' wonderland ' possible that the priestly religion of the Old Testament used ancient and immemorial rites, like the sabbath and the passover, and charged them with new meanings, so that man should enter into communion with God, with his conscience freed (as far as possible) from the intolerable burden of his sin. At the heart of the whole sacrificial system was not a consciously held doctrine of its meaning and of how it affected God, but rather a subconscious sense that it was ordained and commanded by God, obedience to whose revealed will (however dimly perceived or distortedly understood) was of the very essence of man's responsibility.

If the Psalms are the hymn book of the Second Temple, then the reality of the Spirit at the heart of priestly religion is expressed in such phrases as " Whither shall I go from thy spirit ? or whither shall I flee from thy presence ? ",[1] and " Teach me to do thy will ; for thou art my God : let thy good spirit lead me in the land of uprightness ".[2] Here is a glimpse of the true atmosphere of Temple worship, such as we see at its best in the birth stories of John the Baptist and Jesus.[3] The Jewish religion was intended to be a *condominium*, or joint rule by two masters (as by Great Britain and Egypt of the Sudan before its independence), but a *condominium* of prophets and priests is never easy to work. Therefore the downgrading of the prophets soon after the exile is not surprising. But before that happened, there was a moment when the perfect *condominium* of prophets and priests was realized, when the prophets Haggai and Zechariah attempted to translate the priestly vision [4] of the ' ecclesiastical polity ' of the ideal Jerusalem into fact by rebuilding the Second Temple.

It is probably to this period of Jewish history that we should attribute that majestic interpretation of the work

[1] Psalm 139 : 7   [2] Psalm 143 : 10 (margin)
[3] Luke 1, 2   [4] Ezekiel 40–48

of the Creator which we find in Genesis 1. Here in the so-called Priestly Code the whole operation of giving shape and form to the hitherto inchoate universe is attributed to the Spirit of God. Before ever God ' says ' anything, his Spirit ' moves '. This is entirely in accordance with the priority which we have already noticed in the Old Testament of the primitive *ruach* over the prophetic *dabar*. " The spirit of God moved upon the face of the waters ".[1] It is this contact with the great deeps—whether those deeps are in the psychological unconscious or in a cosmic universe beyond our mortal ken—which is the secret of all creativity. It is in the priestly tradition that we find this contact attributed to the Spirit of God, because it is through the priestly tradition that this contact is maintained by the Spirit of God.

*   *   *   *   *

Is there any " fire upon the earth " today, reminiscent of Isaiah's great experience in the Temple, when " one of the seraphim " flew unto him " having a live coal in his hand, which he had taken with the tongs from off the altar " ?[2] We need the fire of the altar as much as Isaiah did. Can we see any contemporary signs of it ? If the fire of the primitive Spirit can be seen in the Revival Movement of East Africa, and the fire of the prophetic Spirit in the Œcumenical Movement, then the fire of the priestly Spirit can certainly be seen in the Liturgical Movement. This is not just a reaction ; there is something creative about it, for priestly symbolism is often more potent to touch the deepest levels of the soul than prophetic words. It can fire our imagination, without offending our aesthetic sensibility.

The Liturgical Movement must be seen against the background of the profound disillusionment of the whole Western world both with Catholicism and with Protestant-

[1] Genesis 1 : 2   [2] Isaiah 6 : 6

ism.[1]   On the one hand there is a widespread dissatisfaction with the incomprehensibility of the traditional symbols of the Christian faith, where these have been preserved unreformed and where they are constantly being embellished with an ever-growing mass of secondary accretions in Catholicism.   The rites of the church are a closed book to the minds of all except the privileged and initiated.   Its language is antique and unrelated, whether in mediæval Latin or Elizabethan English, to any vocabulary of contemporary significance and meaning.

On the other hand, there is also a widespread dissatisfaction with the thin abstraction and theoretical intellectualism of so much modern Protestantism.   It has lost its roots in the primitive, and so without the symbolism of the priest, the prophet has no way of reaching creatively and purposefully the hidden depths of the soul.   This is painfully clear in some parts of the mission field.   We have stripped the soul of Africa naked, and the last state of nominal Christianity may well be worse, unless we are careful, than the first state of real animism or polytheism.   In place of a real religion, however crude and superstitious, we have introduced a theory of religion, which (however refined and highly articulated) is powerless in the face of the elemental forces which it has signally failed to tap, let alone channel into creative and positive experiments in corporate and individual living.

Protestantism is dying through lack of living symbols, and the feverish activities of the artificially stimulated members of its body cannot for ever disguise this fact. Statistically, the non-Christian population of the world is increasing much faster than the Christian.   That is bad enough, and it makes nonsense of the facile and quite futile expectation of the conversion of all (or even

[1] I use the term ' Catholicism ' to include much of high church Anglicanism, and the term ' Protestantism ' to include much of low church Anglicanism.

of a majority of) mankind in the foreseeable future. But what is far worse than this quantitative retreat is the qualitative failure of Protestant Christendom any longer to grip the soul of modern man at the very heart of his existence.

It is not true that a modern understanding of the Bible has increased our awareness of the living God of whom the Bible speaks. It is a plain lie to claim that the removal of idolatry has led to a revival of real religion. On the contrary, it has led to the blatant modern determination to reverence nothing at all as holy—neither church, nor ministry, nor sacrament, nor book, nor day, nor experience. If Archbishop Söderblom was right, the truest touchstone of real religion is not whether we believe in God, or whether we believe in Jesus Christ, but whether we believe in anything at all that is holy. Our modern danger does not seem to be superstition or idolatry so much as atheism, apostasy and infidelity.

How can we combat this danger, which is so very different from that which confronted our forefathers whether in the Bible, or in the so-called ' ages of faith ' or at the Reformation ? We cannot manufacture symbols of the Holy—they could no more grip the depths of the unconscious than can the mere words of the prophetic Spirit, divorced from their primitive roots. Only via the given, and not manufactured, symbol can the creative energies of the primitive and the unconscious again be tapped, and only via these given symbols can the way be opened to that hidden word, or oracle, or *debir*, which lies at the heart of the universe.

But where can these given symbols be found ? There seem to be three possible answers to this question. They may be found in man's ancestral heritage : they may be found in the Christian religion ; and they can be evoked in the modern world to meet modern needs. First, there are the ancient and ancestral religious rites of mankind and the historic non-Christian religions of mankind.

These wait for transposition rather than abolition—though there may be exceptional cases where abolition is necessary—when they are given a deeper or truer meaning by being taken up into the use of the Christian religion. Christmas, as a Christian festival, began like this, and so did many of our other religious rites and ceremonies.

Secondly, there are the special and distinctive badges of our Christian profession and rites of the Christian church. At the very least, holy baptism and the holy eucharist need to come alive in this modern contemporary world. But this is unlikely to happen unless an entirely new and symbolic significance begins again to clothe the persons who administer these sacraments and the words they use and the things they do at their administration. If Dr Dillistone [1] is right in distinguishing between signs (like road signs), which are shorthand ways of securing prompt and immediate action, and symbols (like mathematical formulæ), which are shorthand ways of securing profound and enduring thought, then it is of the latter even more than of the former that we are in need today, and it is only the priest who can give us them.

Just as the artist tries to express something of the hidden word behind everything, the meaning of which he has glimpsed (perhaps momentarily), and give it a more permanent form so that others may, if possible, catch a second-hand glimpse of his first-hand vision, so the priest must express the wonder of God so that something of his reality begins to dawn on those who watch the ritual, see the ceremonies, and share in the liturgy of the church. These things appeal to the emotions and feelings, often affecting them, like a ' subliminal advertisement ', below the level of consciousness, where the limitless resources of the primitive and the elemental are still waiting to be tapped and channelled to creative enterprises.

[1] cf. F. W. Dillistone, *Christianity and Symbolism* (Collins, 1955)

And this raises the question whether there are not, thirdly, other symbols besides those that are traditional and Christian, which could today evoke these otherwise hidden and inaccessible resources of dynamic energy. Mahatma Gandhi began his non-violent civil disobedience movement, out of which in the end came Indian independence, by his famous " Salt March " in 1930. He walked one hundred and fifty miles to the sea at Dandi and there broke a government monopoly by making salt. In so doing he was not only defying an irksome and infuriating law : he was also creating a symbol of independence, round which he could rally Indian resistance against the British *raj* ; and as he once pointed out to a Cornish friend of mine, it is our British failure to understand the need of using symbols that has proved so fatal to our cause, especially in a country as largely illiterate as India. My friend, Mr John Pearce, replied that, being a Cornishman, he agreed wholeheartedly with this, for in Cornwall people still knew the value of symbols. Till this day few of them take sugar in their tea, and this is a tradition that goes back to the time when John Wesley told his followers in Cornwall not to take sugar (from the West Indian plantations) in their tea, as a token or symbol of their refusal to have anything to do with slavery. The important thing about both Mahatma Gandhi's and John Wesley's symbol is that neither of them was artificially manufactured to express a truth. Each expressed naturally a deep and profound truth, and their symbolic expressiveness proved more able to grip the unconscious and subconscious depths of the soul than the most impressive verbal or visual bombardments of consciousness.

It is the function of priestly and corporate religion to hand down the hallowed symbols of antiquity so that their profound meaning may grip the emotions and feelings and the unconscious depths of the soul of contemporary man. It is the function of prophetic and individual religion to rejuvenate these ancient symbols and transform them into living and meaningful expressions of truth, capable of inspiring and challenging the conscious obedience of the will of contemporary man. It is also the prophetic function to seize upon new symbols as they emerge naturally in contemporary life and make them vehicles capable of conveying truth to all levels of the human personality.

If in Jesus Christ there is a perfect blend of the conservative and the radical, there is in his example a clear warrant for the continuance in his church of both the prophetic and the priestly traditions,[1] and a clear warning of the disaster that is sure to follow their divorce. Yet in any community the difficulty of maintaining the proper balance between them is very great. Either the priest is so anxious to hold on to the past that he drives the prophet into rebellion against the past, or the prophet is so anxious to push on to the future that he forces the priest to embalm the past in order to secure its continuance in the present. But neither prophetic rebellion nor priestly stagnation is the answer to the problems of the growing life of any organism. The spiritual sickness of modern man can only be healed if he is given symbols that he can understand. The situation demands two remedies : Protestants must rediscover their symbols ; Catholics must try to understand and, where necessary, simplify them in order to make them comprehensible. It is where both these things are happening that we can see signs of the fire of the altar " upon the earth " today.

In art, architecture, music and above all in the ordering, conduct and ceremonial of the central eucharistic act of Christian worship, profound changes have occurred in the last fifty years over wide sections of Christendom. It

---

[1] Why should the ' finished work ' of the perfect priest rule out the need for other priests, if the ' finished work ' of the perfect prophet does not rule out the need for other prophets ?

is significant, in the light of the present attempt to bring the Church of England and the Church of Scotland into closer relationship, that there should have been recently in the Church of Scotland such a revived interest in worship as has found expression in the *Book of Common Order* and the work of Dr W. D. Maxwell (*An Outline of Christian Worship*, *1936*) and Dr A. A. McArthur (*The Evolution of the Christian Year*, *1953*). At the same time in the Church of England the pioneering venture of Father A. G. Hebert's *Liturgy and Society*, *1935*, has been followed by the stupendous achievement of Dom Gregory Dix's *The Shape of the Liturgy*, *1945*.

These scholarly works have been inspired by or have led to creative experiments in Christian worship which are of revolutionary significance. The papal encyclical of 1903 insisting on " the active participation of the faithful in the holy mysteries " was followed by a whole series of actions by Pope Pius X designed to reform the liturgical practice of the Roman Catholic church ; and the impetus to change, which the Pope thus gave, has been followed by reforms and experiments in both the theory and the practice of Christian worship, which are still going on.

The vernacular mass is now much more popular in the Roman communion than it used to be. Changes have been made in the position of the altar or holy table (now replacing the central rostrum or pulpit in many Protestant churches), and in the position of the celebrant of the eucharist (now facing westward, instead of eastward or at ' the north end ', in many Anglican churches). There has been a restoration of the ancient emphasis on the offertory procession (as in the best tradition of the Orthodox church), and a new insistence on the communion of the people as an integral part of the eucharistic service in churches, where non-communicating attendance at high mass had become common. Perhaps most surprising of all, evening celebrations of the holy communion with official encouragement from Rome have led to the rediscovery by many of the significance of the original evening hour for the central act of Christian worship.

More controversial liturgical developments, combining in a remarkable way primitive, prophetic and priestly elements, have been the attempt by Father Geoffrey Beaumont to compose a Folk Mass with a genuine appeal to the primitive and subconscious, and also the experiments of Canon Southcott at Halton near Leeds, where the communion service, taken to the homes of the people, has been given an entirely new evangelistic intention. Dispute as to whether this agrees with the original intention of our Lord and the practice of the early church should not blind us to the wonderful family life of Halton parish church. Here is a true community at worship, with all the community's needs and activities related to and sanctified by its worship, and with holy baptism restored to something like its original community significance. In many ways Halton exemplifies all that is best in the Parish and People Movement in the Church of England.

There are still fears among Protestants that such expressions of the priestly, as opposed to the prophetic, Spirit are the thin end of the wedge of ' Romanism ', of which some are desperately afraid. But history will not stand still—either for the adulators of the Fathers or for the slavish imitators of the Reformers. The very thing that Protestants were so concerned to abolish at the Reformation—the blocking rather than the opening of the way of the soul to God by the intervention of the priestly ministry—has reappeared in an entirely different form in Protestantism, in which so often the mannerisms, oratory and sometimes exhibitionism of the prophetic ministry are quite as fatal obstacles to the communion of the soul with God as " the mutter of the mass ".

In this connection the development of ritual and the

use of set forms of prayer in Protestant churches is a priestly sign of the times. These may indicate a falling-away from the original sectarian enthusiasm, which made the Quaker meeting and the Evangelical *extempore* prayer meeting the very gate of heaven to those who were privileged to take part in such devotions. But they may also indicate a true movement of the Spirit of God, who is never content to leave any soul or community on a static platform of past achievement but is always pushing it on to new possibilities of spiritual life and growth.

One hundred years ago prophetic Protestantism brought a breath of new spiritual life to the Middle East ; but the ancient priestly churches were very suspicious of it and violently opposed its proselytism. Today those ancient churches are stirring with new life, and the rootlessness of third or fourth generation Protestant converts is often a tragedy. Because Bishop Gobat, in the last century, and Bishop Gwynne, both in the last century and in this, were wonderful missionaries, it does not follow that their work should be a pattern for ours, even if it certainly should be an inspiration to us. The inadequacy of so much Protestant worship to meet the need for colour, life, rhythm and music is clearly apparent to any who are prepared sympathetically to enter into the spirit of the peoples of the Mediterranean and Middle Eastern lands. The individualism of a previous age has provoked the swing of the pendulum towards the communism of our present age. In this situation only a strong church life—and that means a profound work of the priestly Spirit—is adequate either to resist the pressures of secularism and totalitarianism or to satisfy the hunger of the depths of the human soul.

Was it perhaps the Egyptian atmosphere of the Church of Jesus the Light of the World, in Old Cairo, which encouraged a young Coptic monk from the monasteries of Wadi Natrun to come into that church during evensong on one occasion during the last war, and kneel before the altar quite unselfconsciously and in complete disregard of the presence of other worshippers in the church ? It may be that it is only in a truly priestly church that men and women of all classes and ages can feel so naturally at home without the closed bonds of a common clique or the forced bonds of a common fanaticism. The last time I visited the Church of the Holy Sepulchre in Jerusalem I found an Arab family having their lunch in a corner of the Greek *Katholikon*, with their baby slung across the corner of the cathedral in a hammock. They were completely at home. If the church is not the place where we feel naturally at home, is it likely to be the place where we shall find ourselves at home with God ? Nature without grace is not good enough. But un-natural grace is bad. If the former still needs conversion, the latter is an actual perversion.

The prophetic Spirit is not enough : the priestly Spirit is needed too. To appeal to the intellect and the will is one thing : to rouse the emotions and feelings and fire the imagination is another. If the thought of the active life is important, the devotion of the contemplative life is essential. " Those whom God hath joined together, let no man put asunder." But that is just what we have done, and the tragedy of it was brought home forcibly to me one Saturday afternoon in Hamburg two years ago. Seeing a new church, I went in to have a look round. Inside, I found the Lutheran pastor talking about the meaning of its architecture, which was designed to express the Christian faith, with its stone altar in the centre, and a seven-branched candlestick on one side of it, and a pulpit lectern on the other. It was a lecture, and the walls were spotlessly whitewashed, and the clear glass let in all the sunshine of a lovely summer afternoon.

Less than half a mile farther on I saw another church and again stopped and went in. It was later now : the octagonal church (or was it hexagonal?) had stained glass, and the light was dim. No service was going on.

Candles were lit, especially round the statue of the Blessed Virgin Mary, and many men as well as women were praying. This church was also brand new, but its atmosphere in the dim religious light was totally different. If the one was active and appealed to the intellect, the other was contemplative and appealed to the feelings and emotions. Never did I feel more keenly the tragedy of our present church divisions and the total inadequacy of either side of the great Catholic–Protestant 'divide' to give a full expression of the prophetic and priestly wonder of Jesus Christ himself.

CHAPTER IV

THE FIRE OF THE MIND AND THE PHILOSOPHICAL SPIRIT

AFTER the primitive, the prophetic, and the priestly, the
Old Testament evidence for the work of the Spirit moves
to the philosophical. The Exile marks the spiritual
watershed of Israel. In the furnace of national affliction
prophet and priest were welded into a common medium
for the divine revelation. And in the mystical communion of Isaiah 40–66 we seem to have entered a new
world of spiritual achievement, which even the greatest
pre-exilic prophets hardly penetrated at all.

The enforced passivity of exilic conditions in Babylon
encouraged the deep reflection and meditation upon
great spiritual truths, which are impossible so long as the
active endeavour to translate the spiritual vision into
concrete fact fills the energies of all concerned. But in
the hurly-burly of the attempt to restore the Jewish
national life and to rebuild the Jewish national home after
the Exile, such reflection, as in the Exile quite rightly
produced the majestic account of creation in Genesis 1,
easily degenerated into a form of escapism, repetitive,
abstract, theoretical and sterile. This is inevitable if
reflection about the wonder of God is allowed to replace
experience of that wonder, and a self-chosen spectator's
safe point of vantage for observing the divine drama is
preferred to God's appointed post of danger and responsibility as an actor on the stage of the divine drama
itself.

It is in the light of some such evaluation of the post-
exilic scene that we have to assess the contribution made
by the Wisdom literature of the Old Testament and the
Apocrypha to the doctrine of the Spirit of God. First of

all, we must give credit where credit is due. There is a sublime tranquillity about the international character of so much of the Wisdom literature which is a great relief from the intense passions of exclusive nationalism, surging all around. There is a saneness and a spaciousness about its morality—even if this at times seems rather pedestrian after the flights of pure prophetic poetry— which lift us out of the narrow bigotries of ecclesiastical rivalry, which seem so constantly to bedevil the petty actors on the diminutive post-exilic Judæan stage.

But reflection upon the past is no substitute for creative action in the present—and without the continual cross-fertilization of the latter, the former will not remain creative for long : it will soon become merely repetitive. The tragedy of post-exilic Judaism was that the Spirit, who once " spake by the prophets ", now spoke no more through them, and by stifling his operations (by down-grading his agents) the priests deprived themselves also of their own opportunity to open up creative avenues for the Spirit's work. In vain were the sacrifices multiplied and the ritual elaborated. The high priest still went into the Holy of Holies once a year on the Day of Atonement —a majestic and awe-inspiring symbol opening the way to the oracle of God.[1] But the oracle itself had ceased to be a voice : it could only produce an echo. And so complete was this estrangement from the living God that it was with the utter amazement of complete novelty that John the Baptist was acclaimed as " the voice of one crying . . . Make ye ready the way of the Lord ".[2]

Our judgment on this must surely be that as an over-flow of and as a reflection upon the wonder of God, as this had broken through in the primitive, the prophetic, and the priestly traditions of Israel, the philosophical Wisdom literature had great value. It brought together, co-ordinated and harmonized the creative achievements

[1] Ecclesiasticus 50 : 1 ff.
[2] Mark 1 : 3

of the past and, as such, was a necessary prelude to any further spiritual advance. The trouble came when the voluntary pursuit of wisdom became a substitute for or an escape from the pioneering responsibility laid upon man by the wisdom of God.

The greatness of the Wisdom tradition is pre-eminently affirmed in the claim of the prologue to S. John's Gospel that Jesus is the Word, or *logos* of God. But Jesus was not born into the philosophical circles of the Wisdom literature, which in his day may well have been better expressed by Philo and the Jewish colony at Alexandria than by any section of the community in Palestine itself. On the contrary, he was born into a distinctly non-philosophical pietist group connected with the established religion of the day.

Nevertheless, the fact that the philosophical tradition of Proverbs 8 : 22 ff., Wisdom 7 : 22 ff., 9 : 9 ff., and Ecclesiasticus 24 : 1 ff. did not eventually prove to be the matrix of the Son of God should not blind us to the fact that the two most creative and original writers of the New Testament saw in such passages their deepest clue as to the meaning and significance of Jesus Christ. It is this philosophical tradition that is the inspiration of the prologue to S. John's Gospel and of one of Paul's greatest descriptions of Christ.[1]

The combined prophetic and priestly tradition comes to its climax in Zechariah's grand affirmation at the time of the Temple rebuilding, " This is the word of the Lord unto Zerubbabel, saying, Not by might, nor by power, but by my spirit, saith the Lord of hosts. Who art thou, O great mountain ? before Zerubbabel thou shalt become a plain : and he shall bring forth the head stone with shoutings of Grace, grace, unto it." [2] The Mosaic covenant of grace had not yet become completely submerged beneath the post-exilic interpretation of it as a

[1] Colossians 1 : 14 ff.
[2] Zechariah 4 : 6 f.

contract of law. How much trouble Paul would have been spared in his attempt to harmonize Sinai and Calvary, if only he had realized that what he believed to be original Mosaic legislation was very often well-meaning post-exilic invention !

After Zechariah, we look in vain for evidence of the Spirit's contemporary work except in the Wisdom litera-ture. In the rest of Judaism people looked back on his work in the past or they looked forward to his work in the future : they had no experience of his work in the present. He was either a memory or a hope. Zechariah himself looks back to " the words which the Lord of hosts had sent by his spirit by the hand of the former prophets " [1] and the classic expression of the future hopes of Israel is in the passage in Joel's prophecy which Peter took as the text for his sermon on the Day of Pentecost [2] : " It shall come to pass afterward, that I will pour out my spirit upon all flesh ; and your sons and your daughters shall prophesy, your old men shall dream dreams, your young men shall see visions : and also upon the servants and upon the handmaids in those days will I pour out my spirit."

Of the importance of this future hope in post-exilic Judaism there can be no doubt, but a future which is related to the present purely by way of compensation is in danger of degenerating into mere phantasy or wishful thinking. And when we ask for any evidence of that present experience of the Spirit which can link the here and now with the hereafter, we find our only answer in the Wisdom literature and the Psalms connected with it. Here the ' brooding ' Spirit of Genesis 1 : 2 (margin) continues to brood. " Thou sendest forth thy spirit, they are created ; and thou renewest the face of the ground." [3] Even the upstart Elihu can acknowledge that " The

---

[1] Zechariah 7 : 12
[2] Joel 2 : 28 f. : cf. Acts 2 : 17 f. : cf. also Zechariah 12 : 10
[3] Psalm 104 : 30

spirit of God hath made me, and the breath of the
Almighty giveth me life "[1] and Job confesses that the
same Spirit, or *ruach*, is responsible for the beauty[2] of the
heavens.

Finally, wisdom and *ruach* are brought into the closest
possible connection, even if they are not completely
identified, in the profound philosophical passages in the
Wisdom of Solomon. " A holy spirit of discipline will
flee deceit, and will start away from thoughts that are
without understanding, and will be put to confusion when
unrighteousness hath come in. For wisdom is a spirit
that loveth man, and she will not hold a blasphemer
guiltless for his lips ; because God beareth witness of his
reins, and is a true overseer of his heart, and a hearer of
his tongue : because the spirit of the Lord hath filled the
world, and that which holdeth all things together hath
knowledge of every voice." [3] This passage is reinforced
by the claim that there is in wisdom, the artificer of all
things, " a spirit quick of understanding, holy, alone in
kind, manifold, subtil, freely moving, clear in utterance,
unpolluted, distinct, unharmed, loving what is good,
keen, unhindered, beneficent, loving toward man, sted-
fast, sure, free from care, all-powerful, all-surveying, and
penetrating through all spirits that are quick of understanding, pure, most subtil : for wisdom is more mobile
than any motion ; yea, she pervadeth and penetrateth
all things by reason of her pureness ".[4] This majestic
passage goes on and on with a *crescendo* of glorious
descriptions of wisdom as " a breath of the power of
God, and a clear effluence of the glory of the Almighty ;
. . . an effulgence from everlasting light, and an un-
spotted mirror of the working of God, and an image of
his goodness ".[5]

It is true that the early Christians annexed these

---

[1] Job 33 : 4   [2] Job 26 : 13
[3] Wisdom of Solomon 1 : 5–7   [4] Wisdom of Solomon 7 : 22 ff.
[5] Wisdom of Solomon 7 : 25 f.

passages, and others like them, to their interpretation of
Jesus Christ rather than the Holy Spirit. This was a
vital corrective to that tendency towards a sentimental
worship of Jesus, which distorts the revelation of the one
true living God into an idol made in the image of man.[1]
But we must face the fact that, at the time they were first
written and read, these passages were connected with the
Spirit, or *ruach*, of God rather than with the Messiah.
This is made perfectly clear in a text which, most excep-
tionally in pre-Christian literature, brings together the
two terms, 'holy' and 'spirit'. "Who ever," says
Wisdom of Solomon 9 : 17, "gained knowledge of thy
counsel except thou gavest wisdom, and sentest thy holy
spirit from on high ?"

The Spirit in the Wisdom literature is more of a reflec-
tive than an explosive force, and it issues in the Wisdom
of Solomon more in confidence of immortality—"the souls
of the righteous are in the hand of God, and no torment
shall touch them "[2]—than in full-blooded hope of
resurrection. When we turn back to the new covenant,
prophesied by Jeremiah and Ezekiel with the promise,
"a new spirit will I put within you . . . I will put my
spirit within you ",[3] and the vision of the valley of dry
bones, resurrected by the in-breathing of the Spirit of
God,[4] we realize that the fulfilment of these hopes is not
yet. Nevertheless, it was the Wisdom literature that
kept alive in the present experience of post-exilic Jews
the reality of that working of the Spirit of God upon
which the fulfilment of those hopes would ultimately
depend. Furthermore, it is perhaps significant that while
all elements in Judaism were to some extent implicated
in the crucifixion of Jesus Christ, the evidence does not
suggest that the heirs of the Wisdom literature played

---

[1] We badly need the astringent corrective of the antiseptic prologue of
S. John to some of our Christmas sentimentalism.

[2] Wisdom of Solomon 3 : 1

[3] Ezekiel 36 : 26 f.   [4] Ezekiel 37 : 5 (margin)

anything like the same part in that diabolical miscarriage of justice as the nationalist Zealots, pious Pharisees, and worldly Sadducees. It was not because any emphasis in post-exilic Judaism was in itself wrong that Jesus was crucified. Nationalism finds adequate canonical scriptural sanction in Esther and Maccabees, scepticism in Job and Ecclesiastes, piety in Psalms, morality in Proverbs, sex in the Song of Songs, philosophy in the Wisdom literature and ritual in Leviticus—all these are good and wholesome, in their right place and in their proper proportions. As such they—like arsenic—can each make their contribution to the whole. But if they get out of proportion, then—also like arsenic—they are likely to prove fatal. Perhaps the philosophical tradition was too weak to fulfil its proper salty role in the body politic of first century Judaism : certainly the prophetic tradition had ceased to play any significant role. More prophecy was vital, but more philosophy would have helped.

* * * * *

" A flame was kindled in my mind " is what Justin Martyr says in describing his conversion, and the phrase is used as the title of the Bishop of London's Lent book for 1957.[1] Where can we see signs of this " flame in the mind " today ? Whatever we think of the patristic or the mediæval Christian outlook, at least it gave a semblance of unity to the structure of the whole then-known world, which was a great improvement upon our present fragmented worlds, both of thought and life. It is the strong appeal of both Marxism and scientific humanism that each up to a point seems to offer such a unity. And, no matter what their faults, woe betide us if we despise either political or scientific attempts to " see life steadily and to see it whole " ! There is something gloriously free and exhilarating today about the international activity of scientists taking part in the geophysical year,

[1] G. L. Phillips, *Flame in the Mind* (Longmans, 1957)

and of agents of UNESCO, helping in relief work in underdeveloped countries.

But it would seem all-important to recognize and learn from the historical sequence of the Old Testament revelation. The primitive stage comes first, and it cannot be displaced : the prophetic and the priestly come second, and only as an overflow from them does the philosophical stage emerge. Not only does this sharply challenge any attempt to substitute thought for action, but it also emphasizes in the strongest possible manner the fact that any truly creative internationalism springs out of an intense nationalism on its yonder side. There is no possibility of any creative internationalism that has not come through the furnace of nationalist passions. Enthusiasts for the United Nations or the World Council of Churches have precisely nothing to offer to our contemporary spiritual need, if they have lost their own national or denominational roots.

Furthermore, the ethical standards of the Wisdom literature, which are so refreshingly like those of the wider Middle Eastern world and so relatively free from the forced hot-house atmosphere of ecclesiastical bigotries or political passions, are the by-product of the great prophetic achievements of earlier generations. To carry out and apply the implications of the depth of the prophetic revelation, the width of the philosophical interpretation is vital, and the same Spirit inspires both. But the philosophical is no substitute for the prophetic and if it dissociates itself from the priestly, it will soon be involved in that curse of abstraction, which (as Professor Emil Brunner so rightly perceives) is bringing its inevitable judgment upon so much of Western Christendom today.

During the last war I was continually told by Jews in Palestine that they had produced little reflection upon or philosophy about their achievements : they said that the time was not yet ripe for such reflection, because it was fully occupied by action. I felt, and feel, that this may well be a word of salutary warning to those of us who so easily and so fatally allow an increase of knowledge about God to be a substitute for an increase of knowledge of him. Any flowering of the philosophical Spirit can only occur on the yonder side of an outbreak of primitive enthusiasm and prophetic inspiration. If there are signs of these latter two elements of the fully orbed experience of the Holy Spirit today, and if they are balanced by a corresponding priestly emphasis—and this is what the existence of the contemporary Revival, Œcumenical and Liturgical Movements suggests—then we may well look forward to some more synthetic approach towards a new wholeness of life and a revised Christian *weltanschauung*, of which our modern depart-mentalism stands in such sore need.

It was because Augustine and Dante came at the end of great periods of creative thought and achievement that they were able to give their contemporaries such majestic expressions of the philosophical Spirit. The time for such a philosophy may not yet be ripe. But perhaps we can catch glimmerings of light, pointing towards a future integration of our contemporary chaos of thought and action. In the twentieth century it would be hard to deny the inspiration of the philosophical Spirit to such Gifford lecturers as Archbishop Söderblom of Sweden, Archbishop William Temple of Great Britain and Dr Reinhold Niebuhr of the United States of America. Perhaps the two archbishops will in the end be ranked as greater than Dr Niebuhr, not because they had an ecclesiastical dignity which he had not, but because they were prepared to run the risk of heresy by contamination with syncretism in the one case and with liberalism in the other in a way that he was not.

The point in question is not trivial. Professor Karl Barth's tremendous theological challenge to con-temporary thought started (in his own words) as a

" question mark " in the margin of the works of those he criticized. Is it impertinent to put a similar question mark in the margin of his own work ? Undoubtedly he spoke as a prophet in his great commentary on the Epistle to the Romans. Undoubtedly, too, he has realized the contemporary need for a comprehensive philosophy to bring sense and order into the dismembered fragments of our ancient Christian wholeness of outlook. But is the philosophy, of which we are in need, possible without more cross-fertilization of the biblical tradition with extra-biblical insights into the wonder of the truth of God than Karl Barth is willing to allow?

It may be that it is his awareness of Dr Karl Barth's limitations in this respect that has caused Professor Rudolf Bultmann to attempt to penetrate through the biblical thought forms (so many of which he would discard) to the essential biblical gospel. If Barth is afraid lest modern secular ideas should get between us and a true understanding of the gospel, Bultmann is equally afraid of ancient biblical ideas—and for precisely the same reason. That there were grounds for Barth's fear in the liberal theology of the 1920s I should whole-heartedly agree : but I should also agree that there are now grounds for Bultmann's fear in some trends of biblical theology in the 1950s.

In order to express the true wholeness of life and thought, the philosophical Spirit permits a man neither to deny the depth of his own individual heritage nor to ignore the challenge of other traditions than his own. Life comes by intercourse or cross-fertilization, and truth by dialectic or conversation. Any present-day Christian expression of the philosophical Spirit is bound to be up against the same danger as faced the post-exilic Jewish wise men, the early Christian Fathers, and the scholastic philosophers of the Middle Ages—the danger, i.e., of losing the essential uniqueness of the biblical revelation in a vague and universal syncretism.

The philosophical Spirit may not have been able to find a wholly Christian expression through the influence of Plato, Vergil and Aristotle upon Augustine, Dante and Aquinas, but without their influence it is doubtful whether that Spirit, confined solely to the biblical tradition, would have found any expression at all.   Cross-fertilization is very dangerous, but it is essential, and it found expression in the Wisdom literature in the teeth of the intense opposition of the fanatical exclusiveness of most of post-exilic Judaism.

Therefore we have scriptural warrant for including in our search for evidences of the philosophical Spirit in our own day not only the work of Father Wilhelm Schmidt on comparative religion, but also such dangerously syncretistic systems as the psychology of Professor C. G. Jung and the history of Professor Arnold Toynbee.   No dissatisfaction with their systems should blind us to true insights of the philosophical Spirit which they may contain.

In modern Western universities the science of comparative religion is no longer merely theoretical.   Students not committed to any religion feel that Christianity is by no means the only living option.   While (they feel) Christianity has divided Ireland and not united Western Europe, communism appears to have united Eastern Europe.   President Nasser certainly hopes that Islam will provide the cement to unite something bigger than the Arab world.   U Nu, the Prime Minister of Burma, claims that Buddhism can provide the inspiration for a new internationalism in South-East Asia.   Christians, who have heard the broadcasts of Prince Chula of Thailand, may feel that his preference for Buddhism to Christianity is based upon an inadequate understanding of the essence of Christianity ; but they can well listen, after two world wars, with great humility to the lessons which he thinks Buddhism has to teach Christianity upon the virtue of toleration which seems to be in as short supply in our Western world today as it was in post-exilic Judaism long ago.

Unless the philosophical Spirit forces Christians to recognize and rejoice in the things we have in common with those who do not share our faith, we shall be in danger of the same eventually sterile bigotry and fanaticism that blinded the Jews to their Messiah when he appeared to them. And no amount of missionary enthusiasm or biblical theology will avail us now, if this is the case, any more than it availed them then. The words of Jesus remain as true today of some Christian Bible students and foreign missionaries as they were when they were first spoken of some Jewish Bible students and foreign missionaries. " Ye search the scriptures, because ye think that in them ye have eternal life . . . and ye will not come to me." [1]   " Ye compass sea and land to make one proselyte ; and when he is become so, ye make him two-fold more a son of hell than yourselves." " Woe unto you ! " [2]   All such devoted Bible study and fervent missionary evangelism, however unconscious its hypocrisy, needs a salutary dose of the salty scepticism, worldly wisdom, and profound, but reverent, agnosticism of so much of the great Wisdom literature of all ages. Would that there were more of it today ! And would that those who need its salutary corrective to their over-dogmatism and forced enthusiasm would listen to what there is !

[1] John 5 : 39 f.   [2] Matthew 23 : 15 f.

CHAPTER V

THE FIRE OF THE HEART AND THE PIETIST SPIRIT

PERHAPS we are wrong to say that reminiscence about the past, expectation of the future and reflection on the present comprise all that post-exilic Judaism knew of the Spirit of God. For there were pockets of resistance against the fanaticism and shallow secularism of the time, oases of deep piety such as we find in S. Luke 1, 2. Although this particular group of people had been chosen for an exceptional task, there is no reason to suppose that there were not other similar groups.

Pietism, with its distinctive witness to the present reality and wonder of the living God, is the seed-bed of much of the creative spiritual inspiration of the world. It is not without significance that the birth stories of Jesus in S. Matthew 1, and of Jesus and John the Baptist in S. Luke 1, 2, bring back into circulation that vocabulary of the Spirit which had been so sparingly used in post-exilic Judaism. Whatever view we take of the historicity of these birth stories, they are clear evidence for first century belief that at this point in human history God took a new creative initiative. Just as the Spirit was active in the world's creation,[1] so the Holy Spirit (the two words are now used together) was supremely active in its re-creation.

This is the significance of the new vocabulary. There were experiences which demanded an explanation—the Holy Spirit was the explanation which S. Luke (and, to a lesser degree, S. Matthew) offered of those experiences. But even more important than the experiences, as psychological and spiritual happenings, was the conviction of

[1] Genesis 1 : 2

63

the New Testament writers that with the herald pro-
clamation of John the Baptist and the birth of Jesus himself the new longed-for Messianic era had actually
dawned. His birth was to them an ' eschatological '
event. It belonged to the ' last things ' and would not,
like everything else, be upset or turned topsy-turvy by
those ' last things '. Because of their conviction of the
dawn of the Messianic age, the New Testament writers
were sure of the outpouring of the Holy Spirit. The
great expectations of the Messiah's birth were bound
up with the great expectations of the Spirit's work, and
the connection was indissoluble.

Therefore it is with no surprise that we find S. Matthew
attributing the conception of Jesus to the work of the
Holy Spirit. " Now the birth of Jesus Christ was on this
wise : When his mother Mary had been betrothed to
Joseph, before they came together, she was found with
child of the Holy Ghost." [1] This explanation of her
conception is reinforced by the angelic message in a
dream to Joseph, which categorically states that " that
which is conceived in her is of the Holy Ghost ".[2]
S. Matthew's birth story is otherwise so strikingly different
from S. Luke's that their joint testimony to a special
creative intervention of the Holy Spirit is most impressive.
And we are not surprised to find that S. Luke, the companion of Paul—with all his vivid experience of the work
of the Holy Spirit in the Gentile missionary church—
elaborates and expands S. Matthew's two brief references.
For S. Luke, John the Baptist also is to " be filled with
the Holy Ghost, even from his mother's womb ",[3] and
the words of the Annunciation tremble with the unbelievable expectation of the incarnation : " The Holy Ghost
shall come upon thee, and the power of the Most High
shall overshadow thee : wherefore also that which is to
be born shall be called holy, the Son of God." [4]

[1] Matthew 1 : 18   [2] Matthew 1 : 20
[3] Luke 1 : 15   [4] Luke 1 : 35

In S. Luke not only Mary, but Elisabeth also is " filled with the Holy Ghost ",[1] and old Simeon's prophetic and providential appearance on the scene of the Purification is linked in the closest possible way with the work of the Holy Spirit. " The Holy Spirit was upon him " . . . " it had been revealed to him by the Holy Spirit that he should not see death before he had seen the Lord's Christ " . . . " he came in the Spirit into the temple ".[2] With these explicit references to the Holy Spirit should be linked the prophetic songs, embedded in these narratives, which perhaps more than anything else have represented all down church history the genuine utterance of the Holy Spirit at the heart of Christian worship : Magnificat,[3] Benedictus [4] and Nunc Dimittis.[5]   It was Mary's (or Elisabeth's) " spirit " which rejoiced [6] and Zacharias' inspiration and Simeon's prophecy are directly attributed to the Holy Spirit.[7]

The cumulative evidence of these references powerfully reinforces the central conviction of the Lukan narrative that Jesus' conception was the work of the Holy Spirit by setting it in a context in which the Spirit is transparently and vividly active in the life of this little pietist group and all its individual members. In this community there is liberty for God to work. He is not shackled to the precedents of the past, or restricted to the conventions of the present, or limited to the wishful thinking of the future. He is a present reality, often spoken about because constantly experienced.

The characteristics of this pietist group seem to be threefold. First, though recognizably different from the conventional established religion of the time, this community was not divorced from that religion : on the contrary, it lived in the closest relationship with it and shared its worship. This connection is made very clear by the fact that Zacharias was a priest and received his vision when he was doing his Temple duty " in the order of his course ".[1] Simeon's intervention occurred when Joseph and Mary and Jesus came up to the Temple for the Purification,[2] and his prophetic words were underlined by Anna the " prophetess ",[3] who gave herself up entirely to unbroken worship in the Temple. Twelve years later the Temple was the setting [4] of Jesus' own decisive break-out of the traditional restrictions of the piety in which he had been brought up.

Secondly, this pietist group was not only linked in the closest possible way with the institutional church in the present : it was also filled with the most vivid apocalyptic expectations of the future. The *fait accompli* of the divine visitation [5] was the fulfilment of the intense yearning and longing which filled these simple believers, who were " looking for the consolation of Israel "[6] and " the redemption of Jerusalem ".[7] We can well imagine to what a pitch of vivid hope of imminent deliverance every passover meal—especially in Jerusalem—must have stimulated those who lived in such an atmosphere of expectation.

Thirdly, the piety of this group was not nourished merely on the hope of a compensatory future, designed to make up by its unimaginable spiritual wealth of divine blessings for the undeniable spiritual poverty of present experience. On the contrary, the present experience of these pietists was shot through with contemporary interventions of the living God. No one who reads S. Luke 1, 2 can fail to see how transparent this Jerusalem world was to the eternal world of God. And, while this is no direct evidence as to the atmosphere of Jesus'

[1] Luke 1 : 8
[2] Luke 2 : 22
[3] Luke 2 : 36
[4] Luke 2 : 46
[5] Luke 1 : 68
[6] Luke 2 : 25
[7] Luke 2 : 38

Nazareth home, it strongly suggests that we shall not be wrong if we see simple piety of this Jerusalem pattern as the basic private foundation and ground-work of all Jesus' subsequent public ministry.

There is an other-worldliness about this atmosphere which irresistibly reminds us of Jesus' own categorical assertion that childlikeness is the indispensable *sine qua non* of entering the kingdom of God.[1] He was surely here speaking of something which it had been his priceless privilege to share in his own home from his youngest days. Whether he spoke of the Spirit or not, whether Joseph and Mary spoke of the Spirit or not, the reality of God within the soul[2] and of his interventions in the daily circumstances of everyday life is stamped ineffaceably upon the birth stories both of S. Matthew and S. Luke. In such a context the dogma that Jesus was himself " conceived by the Holy Ghost " becomes a natural expression for the way in which ' the Son ' and not ' the sport ' of God was born. The fact that he himself should have completely transcended the circumstances and spiritual environment of his home and upbringing should not blind us to his dependence upon the human matrix out of which he was born and in which he grew up. Yet on the other hand, if he could in fact only have been born into the world of historic Judaism, it was the hide-bound traditional red-tape of that world, which engineered his death. So near is the height of spiritual greatness to the depth of spiritual degradation. And the point can be made even more significant. If Jesus could only have been born into a simple pietist community within the wider context of the whole of Judaism, he was not able to live except by breaking out of that community. He could only do his Father's will by breaking his mother's heart.[3] Pietism is

[1] Matthew 18 : 3
[2] cf. H. H. Farmer, *Revelation and Religion*, pp. 66 ff.
[3] Luke 2 : 48 f.

indispensable to the continuity of a living experience of the Holy Spirit. But pietism is not all that is indispensable, and if it tries to claim any exclusive monopoly of the Spirit, it proves itself the most fatal enemy of the Spirit.

The pietism of S. Luke 1, 2 was not exclusive. It had the closest ties with the traditional Temple devotion of a Pharisaic rather than a Sadducean type. This is so reassuring to conventional churchmanship that it is very easy to ignore the fact that its contacts may well have been almost equally close with the sectarian piety of the Essenes. It is not yet clear what will be the final evaluation of the significance of the Dead Sea Scrolls, but the immediate proximity of the monastery of Qumran to the scene of John the Baptist's revival campaign seems to demand some close connection between the two. If this is established, then there is a possibility of a threefold stage, whereby the Old Testament piety revealed in S. Luke 1, 2 was converted into the holiness of Jesus Christ. First, pietism connected with conventional churchmanship was exchanged for pietism of a more sectarian type, if John threw in his lot with the covenanters of Qumran. Then secondly, this sectarian piety was exchanged by John the Baptist for a radically ethical prophetism. He was determined not to keep aloof from the sins of the world, but rather to tackle those sins in the world. Thirdly, this radically ethical prophetism was exchanged by Jesus for his own unique mission. He did not merely patronize John's revival : he threw in his lot with him unreservedly. But then, to John's complete bewilderment,[1] he proceeded to pass beyond his cousin's wonderful ministry to fulfil his own unique Messianic vocation.

While pietism has an essential role to play in maintaining the spiritual life of any community, it is important to realize that that role is at two removes from the

[1] Luke 7 : 18 ff.

creative achievement of Jesus Christ himself. Without such a true appraisal of their role and the salutary recognition of their own limitations necessarily involved in it, pietists will always be in danger of making those exclusive claims to spirituality, which are as fatal to themselves as to the community among which they live. Such claims prevent them from exercising any effective influence upon the community, and they cause the community to despise and ignore the very thing it most needs for its own continued spiritual health. Pietism, like patriotism, " is not enough ", but it may well be the prerequisite of almost everything else. Jesus did not remain a member of a pietist group, but he was born into one. We shall not adequately explain the significance of his death if we do not do justice to all the circumstances of his birth.

* * * * *

" I felt my heart strangely warmed " are perhaps the most significant words in all John Wesley's Journal. They remind us vividly of how the first disciples " said one to another, Was not our heart burning within us, while he spoke to us in the way ? " [1] What happened on the first Easter Day during an Old Testament Bible study on the road to Emmaus happened on May 14th, 1738, during a Bible study on the Epistle to the Romans, in Aldersgate Street in London. It did not happen during a service in the established church, although John Wesley tells us that he had been deeply moved by the anthem in St Paul's Cathedral the day before. It happened at a pietist meeting, and it was typical of the inspiration which has come in similar ways all down the history of the church from the day when *Magnificat* was first sung to the present time.

It is not the task of the composer of *Magnificat* to translate into terms of contemporary social and political

[1] Luke 24 : 32

life the utterly revolutionary implications of that true Workers' Charter and genuine *Internationale* of the proletariat. That is for others to do, and they are without excuse if they go on singing its revolutionary words without making any resolute attempt to translate its challenge into terms of contemporary action in the social and political scene. But they may never have the incentive even to attempt to do this unless out of a pietist and other-worldly circle comes their initial inspiration. To hear a genuinely humble Plymouth Brother lead a Crusader Class is not necessarily to be persuaded of the rightness of his theology, but it is undeniably to be deeply impressed by the fact that he may have much more of the " one thing needful " than many of his more worldly-wise and ecclesiastically informed contemporaries. So much missionary enterprise, whether Catholic or Protestant, owes its origin to such pietist inspiration that it would be a major tragedy if those who have outgrown its restricted and circumscribed outlook should either despise or ignore its abiding significance and inspiration.

But three things are vital, if Christian pietism is still to be—as it still can be—the matrix of creative achievements of the Holy Spirit. It must be in a living relationship with traditional organized Christianity : it must look forward to something beyond itself ; and it must have some present insight into the reality of its future hopes. If it divorces itself from its environment, and especially from its religious environment, it will harden into a bigoted fanaticism. If it has no future expectation, it will tend to a complacently selfish cultivation of a highly selective ' spiritual life ', largely of its own imagination. If its future hopes have no comparable balance in present experience, it will rapidly degenerate into visionary and fantastic day-dreaming about what will be, and not make the least attempt to tackle the drudgery of the task which is the indispensable prerequisite of the realization of those dreams.

Precisely these three qualities marked the small Evangelical groups, out of which so much of the modern Protestant missionary movement sprang, and which have been its life blood until the present day. And this work of the pietist Spirit is no Evangelical or Protestant prerogative, for just as John Wesley's fire of the heart influenced Protestantism, so the same fire in the founders of some of the great monastic orders influenced Roman Catholicism.[1] Indeed, Methodism and monasticism have much in common !

The pietist Spirit has found expression in our day in cell movements, like that of the Servants of Christ the King in the Anglican church. It has gone on inspiring the more conservative Evangelical missionary work of the church through the great Keswick Convention in England and parallel activities in other parts of the world, and much of the finest inter-denominational work of the church has been powerfully influenced by it. Via Keswick the pietist Spirit produced the foreign missionary work of Amy Wilson Carmichael at Dohnavur in South India ; and a similar Spirit inspired the creation of *ashrams* in India, such as those associated with the names of Mahatma Gandhi, C. F. Andrews, and Stanley Jones. In contrast to the monastic return to mediæval forms and traditional Catholic interpretations of holiness, there have emerged other and quite different experiments of devotion, which seem at first sight more worldly, but often prove on closer inspection to be perhaps even more truly creative and sacrificial. To be present in the ancient chapel of St Cedd on the coast of Essex at Bradwell-on-Sea and to be ministered to by an ex-communist at evening prayers, with someone in tears nearby in the same row of chairs, was to realize how deep could be the pietist Spirit of the Rev. Norman Motley's experiment of Othona.

The same deep devotion lies behind the work of the

[1] cf. Maximin Piette, *John Wesley in the Evolution of Protestantism* (Sheed & Ward, 1937)

Brethren and other simple Evangelical and often strongly
fundamentalist groups, which the contemporary ' great
church ' should not despise or ignore. When learning
looks down upon holiness the age of intellectual sterility
is in sight, for again and again it is in the simple piety
and holiness of one generation that we find the secret of
great creative intellectual and artistic achievements in
the next. It is not the dogmatic fundamentalism of the
Inter-'Varsity Fellowship but its deep devotional piety
which makes it so powerful an influence in student circles
in Great Britain today. The same is true of the work of
the Crusader movement and other missionary societies,
like the China Inland Mission, the Africa Inland Mission,
the Sudan Interior Mission, the Worldwide Evangelization Crusade and their innumerable counterparts which
flourish (or sometimes languish) on this side and, still
more, on the other side of the Atlantic.

And is there any better description of the pietist Spirit
at its best, whether in Catholic or Protestant circles, than
the moving, but entirely fanciful, story of the adventures
of a Savoyard Franciscan friar in England, written by
Cicely Hallack and published under the title of *The
Happiness of Father Happé* ? [1] Here is the childlike inno-
cence which, when it goes hand in hand with true learning, produces such an irresistible demonstration of the
power of the Spirit of God as to be the nearest approach
we can find anywhere on earth to the sort of environment into which Jesus was once born and out of which
alone perhaps he could be born again.

To provide the opportunity for such a ' re-incarnation '
(if I may call it so) is perhaps the highest ideal at which
any Christian group, society or individual can aim.
" Behold, the handmaid of the Lord ; be it unto me
according to thy word " [2] : no higher vocation is humanly
conceivable, yet no doubt there were in the first century

[1] C. Hallack, *The Happiness of Father Happé* (Browne & Nolan, 1938)
[2] Luke 1 : 38

those who despised the piety of the little group into which our Lord was born. Alas, they have their counterparts in the twentieth century today. The pietist Spirit which we so badly need cannot live in a soul or community where there is any attitude of patronizing condescension towards others or any despising of their naïve and childish attitude to modern life and learning. It was, after all, " unlearned and ignorant men " [1] who first turned the world upside down, and none of us is likely to improve upon their apostolic achievement.

[1] Acts 4 : 13

CHAPTER VI

THE MISSIONARY FIRE AND THE PENTECOSTAL SPIRIT

IF we allow the traditional three years for his public ministry—and critical research would be inclined to shorten rather than to lengthen this period—then Jesus only moved finally out of the pietist environment of his birth and boyhood three years before the outpouring of the Holy Spirit on the Day of Pentecost. So it is best to study the Pentecostal Spirit after the pietist Spirit, leaving till later the evidence of the Gospels and the doctrine of the Paraclete.

The sequence is important because, when the Pentecostal and Pauline evidence for the Holy Spirit is studied after the evidence of the four Gospels, it is so often interpreted as an improvement upon them, as if it demonstrated a higher level of spirituality than they do. This may lead to a fatally distorted view of the way the Holy Spirit works. For he never seeks to improve upon Jesus himself, however many new and hitherto unexpected facets of Jesus' holiness he may be able to reveal. The climax of the Holy Spirit's work in the Bible is seen in the life and ministry and, above all, in the death and resurrection of Jesus Christ himself. There can be no improvement upon him : he is the complete revelation of God.

But the completeness of his revelation can only rightly be appreciated if we approach the plateau of the four Gospels via the ascending slopes of the Acts and the Epistles. " No more certain statement," says Dr C. K. Barrett,[1] " can be made about the Christians of the first generation than this : they believed themselves to be

[1] *The Holy Spirit and the Gospel Tradition* (S.P.C.K., 1947), p. 1

living under the immediate government of the Spirit of God. After various necessary preliminaries, the most ancient book of church history opens with a formal account of the inspiration of the disciples for their task, when, on the Day of Pentecost, the Holy Spirit descended upon them in tongues of flame.[1] The note so impressively struck at the outset is not subsequently changed. There is hardly a chapter of the book in which the Spirit is not represented as at work. Every critical point in the church's history, as here described, is made the scene of the Spirit's intervention. Thus, when the seven ' deacons ' were appointed, it was laid down that they should be men full of the Spirit.[2] When Paul, in process of conversion and preparation for his mission, waited obediently at Damascus, Ananias was sent to him in order that he might receive the Holy Spirit.[3] When Peter first preached to the Gentiles, it was at the Spirit's command ; and that he had rightly understood his instructions was indicated by a repetition of the event of Pentecost for the benefit of Cornelius and his circle.[4] The most critical point of the whole story—the separation of Paul and Barnabas for the purpose of undertaking missionary work of a far wider scope than any that the original disciples had attempted—is recorded in these words : ' The Holy Ghost said, Separate me Barnabas and Saul. . . . So they, being sent forth by the Holy Ghost, went down to Seleucia.' [5] So the decrees ascribed to the apostles and elders in council are introduced by the clause, ' It seemed good to the Holy Ghost, and to us ' [6]; and the route of Paul's journeys in Asia Minor, and his determination to make the decisive journey to Jerusalem, are attributed to the influence of the Spirit.[7] It is clear that

---

[1] Acts 2 : 1–4   [2] Acts 6 : 3, 5
[3] Acts 9 : 17
[4] Acts 10 : 19 f., 44–47 ; 11 : 12, 15 f.
[5] Acts 13 : 2, 4   [6] Acts 15 : 28
[7] Acts 16 : 6 f. ; 19 : 21 ; 20 : 22 f.

the author of Acts thought of the history of the church,
at least in its early days, as governed from first to last by
the Spirit of God."

This lengthy, but impressive, testimony to the complete dominance of the early church by the Holy Spirit
links on quite naturally with his recorded activity at the
time of Jesus' birth. The difference between the Lukan
birth stories and the record of Acts is not that we have
in the former a pre-Christian intermittent impersonal
Spirit and in the latter a Christian permanent personal
Spirit. It is, rather, that in the former the sphere of the
Spirit's work is limited to the highly selective cross section
of life represented by a small pietist group, whereas in
the latter there is no limit to the range of life represented
by the early Christians, who were wide open to all the
currents of contemporary thought and all the challenges
of contemporary events. The pietist clique has become
the Christian church : and the measure of the difference
between the two is the difference between the recorded
activities of the Holy Spirit in each of them.

The hall-mark of these activities is the breaking out of
convention and custom on the yonder side. Not in the
least confined to individuals, the outpouring of the Holy
Spirit at Pentecost was upon a whole community, regardless of differences of age and sex, and even probably of
race and culture as well. This was not anything as
spectacularly novel as some Christian commentators
imagine, nor has it in its recorded Pentecostal exhibition
any necessary ethical quality differentiating it from the
mass hysteria of the frenzied bands of prophets, roaming
about in the pre-monarchical stage of Israelite history.[1]
On the contrary, the first characteristic of the Pentecostal
Spirit is its apparent identity, in ecstatic and abnormal
behaviour, and in its links with an intensely nationalist
outlook,[2] with the earliest primitive stage of the Old
Testament demonstration of the Spirit's work.

[1] cf. 1 Samuel 10 : 10 ff.   [2] cf. Acts 1 : 6

There are, however, two great differences : in Acts this strange behaviour goes hand in hand with belief in the advent of the Messianic age in the person of the Messiah, Jesus, crucified, risen, ascended and now both Lord and Christ. It also creates the pre-condition of a common basis of a new international community by breaking out on both sides of the great 'divide' of the ancient world, the " middle wall of partition " between Jews and Gentiles. Not all abnormal behaviour can be attributed to the Pentecostal Spirit, but only that which is accompanied both by belief in Jesus as Messiah and also by active attempts to break down those barriers which divide men from each other.

The pre-eminent achievement of the Pentecostal Spirit was to break across the great barrier between Jews and Gentiles. In Christ, as Paul realized more clearly than any other apostle, " there cannot be Greek and Jew, circumcision and uncircumcision, barbarian, Scythian, bondman, freeman ".[1] Indeed, he goes even further, and says " there can be neither Jew nor Greek, there can be neither bond nor free, there can be no male and female ".[2] (This final denial of any distinction between the sexes makes it quite clear that Paul is not denying any differences in nature because he is asserting that there is no distinction in grace.)

The work of the Pentecostal, and by no means exclusively Pauline, Spirit was to achieve this unity in Christ out of those who were sundered and separated by the deepest possible hereditary and traditional divisions. The internationalism of the Christian church, which first dawned on the horizon on the Day of Pentecost, was not achieved by by-passing the intense devotion and even fanaticism of nationalism. Across the frontiers of passionately held exclusive loyalties the new community in Christ extended its scope under the manifest and undeniable inspiration of the Holy Spirit. It is a

[1] Colossians 3 : 11   [2] Galatians 3 : 28

magnificent achievement, and we can trace in it almost all those signs of how the Holy Spirit works, which we have previously examined.

First, Pentecost itself is proof positive of the continual need for the Holy Spirit to break up the great deeps of the unconscious. Of the primitive character of the ecstasy, certainly connected with the tongues of fire [1] and probably also connected with the speeches in " other tongues " [2], there can be no doubt at all. Secondly, of the prophetic character of the Spirit's work there is abundant proof not only in Peter's sermon on the Day of Pentecost, but also in his whole handling of the Cornelius' incident and in the initiation of the Gentile missionary movement. But this prophetic element in Acts is balanced, as Protestants so easily ignore, by the definitely sacramental and priestly way in which in two dramatic cases at Samaria [3] and Ephesus [4] the absence of any manifest experience of the Holy Spirit is put right by the laying on of apostolic hands. In both cases the sequel to the sacramental act is, as Catholics so easily forget, the same —visible, obvious and undeniable evidences of the presence and power of the Holy Spirit.

Primitive, prophetic and priestly elements in the tradition of the Holy Spirit are all blended in the Acts of the Apostles. As for the philosophical element, it finds no finer expression in the New Testament than the way in which S. Luke composed his history of the early church in order to preserve church unity, and the way in which Paul wrestled, as, e.g. at Athens,[5] with the problem of finding an adequate evangelistic and apologetic terminology with which to commend the Jewish gospel to the Gentile world. And who can deny that, whenever and wherever the Bethlehem story became known, its pietist Spirit was re-born and lived on, trans-

---

[1] Acts 2 : 3   [2] Acts 2 : 4
[3] Acts 8 : 14 ff.   [4] Acts 19 : 1 ff.
[5] Acts 17 : 22 ff.

formed, as the secret source of inspiration of every little local *ecclesia*, or church, throughout the Mediterranean world ?

The story of Acts is the story of the stupendous missionary achievement of a community inspired to make a continual series of creative experiments by the Pentecostal Spirit. Against a static church, unwilling to obey the guidance of the Holy Spirit, no ' gates ' of any sort are needed to oppose its movement, for it does not move. But against a church that is on the move, inspired by the Pentecostal Spirit, neither " the gates of hell " nor any other gates can prevail. " Nothing can stop it now."

*   *   *   *   *

" Tongues . . . of fire " [1] may be understandable in heaven, where God " maketh his angels winds and his ministers a flame of fire ".[2] They are certainly unaccountable " upon the earth ", and so were all the sights which authenticated the missionary movement of the Pentecostal Spirit across the barriers of the ancient world. But some of the sounds were quite different : they were understandable. If what was seen at Pentecost caused amazement because it was incomprehensible, what was heard caused greater amazement because it was intelligible, for " they were all amazed and marvelled, saying, . . . We do hear them speaking in our tongues the mighty works of God ".[3]

The " tongues . . . of fire " were visible signs of the presence " upon the earth " of the Pentecostal Spirit, the audible evidence of whose activity was the transformation of a foreign language into the vernacular of " our tongues ". Thus on the Day of Pentecost, as on Christmas Day, but in another form, " the Word became flesh, and dwelt among us, and we beheld his glory ".[4] The birthday

---

[1] Acts 2 : 3   [2] Hebrews 1 : 7
[3] Acts 2 : 7 ff.   [4] John 1 : 14

of the church and the start of the Christian missionary movement were not marked by a spectacular display of gibberish, but by an astonishing indication of the lengths to which the Pentecostal Spirit was prepared to carry the principle of identification, enshrined at the heart of the incarnation. The way God broke down the barrier between heaven and earth in Jesus Christ was the way the Pentecostal Spirit broke down the barrier between Jews and Gentiles in the " body " of Christ. In each case there is an identification, and the sort of things that previously happened only on one side of the barrier now happen on both sides, and so the one community of the body of Christ is formed across the barrier, breaking down the " middle wall of partition ".

It was because Peter and Paul saw the signs of the Pentecostal Spirit on the other side of the " middle wall of partition " that they felt obliged to open their fellowship to the Gentiles. That did not mean that they broke out of an intolerant nationalism into a vague internationalism, denying the reality of its nationalist roots, but rather that they were willing to recognize and rejoice in evidence of experiences, comparable with their own, occurring among other peoples beyond their frontiers. If Acts is to be our guide, we dare not fly in the face of facts in order to preserve our national, racial, cultural or ecclesiastical exclusiveness : we are forced to acknowledge our oneness in Christ at the deepest levels of experience with those of other backgrounds and outlooks.

This acknowledgment was not made in Acts by the church as a whole or by an ecclesiastical council or committee. In the first instance it was made by an individual—he happens to have been not only an apostle, but the leader of the apostles ; but there is no reason why he should have belonged to the apostolic band at all. Because of what Peter and Paul had done, a church council was called, and it ratified their actions. But only if the hazardous creative individual experiment (under the guidance of the Holy Spirit) had preceded the church council, called to deal with it, would there have been any chance of that council rightly claiming for its own decision the direction of the Holy Spirit.[1]

The danger of irresponsible individual action is very great : but the danger of avoiding all individual action by insisting on prior reference to authority is even greater. If wrong experiments are harmful, no experiments are fatal. This is a truth for all life, and we never get to the end of its implications till death itself effects the last break with the past and so opens up the possibility of the full glory of the future. The tragedy is that so often those who have behind them the inspiration of the pietist Spirit fail to follow the guidance of the Pentecostal Spirit, who will constantly lead them out of their restricted cliques and stereotyped patterns of behaviour and doctrine into ever new ventures and alignments. To settle down complacently within any one grouping or outlook is suicidal, no matter how fervent our activities within and on behalf of that group.

Yet, this is just what so often happens. The fundamentalist *internationale* has broken down the walls of national and ecclesiastical division only to build up even more divisive walls of doctrinal and moral separation. The work of M.R.A., or the Oxford Group, has similarly achieved much in the international and inter-racial field, only at the cost of imposing a stereotyped conception of guidance, more capable of producing regimental uniformity than organic union. Even the Œcumenical Movement, having broken down so many barriers between different churches and confessions, seems sometimes quite willing to harden against pietists and fundamentalists, as if their opposition to it justified its opposition (except in love) to them. There is real

[1] Acts 15 : 28

danger of breaking down one " wall of partition " and only thereby building up another.

It is impossible to follow the guidance of the Pentecostal Spirit and still adopt the principle of ' thus far and no further '. The principle of identification must be carried through to all lengths. A particularly tragic illustration of the failure to do this is to be seen in the way in which the modern missionary movement has on the whole shirked the deepest, and quite inescapable, implication of carrying out this principle. It is almost unbelievable, if it is true, that such an heroic missionary as Hudson Taylor, who insisted on living as far as possible as the Chinese did, wearing their clothes and even their *queue*, should yet have laid down categorically that no European or American member of the China Inland Mission should marry a Chinese. Such a refusal makes complete mockery of the claim of foreign missionary identification with the people of China, and it contradicts the whole principle of the incarnation.

May not this attitude, so common throughout the mission field, have been one strong reason for the comparative failure of the Christian missions in China to withstand the challenge of communism ? No one would want to belittle missionary heroism in China during the Boxer rebellion right on up till the final expulsion of missionaries by the triumphant communists, but the great heroisms are often not so costly as the humdrum crosses that are put in our path. It is here that the autobiography of Pearl Buck seems strangely significant. Why was it that she was afraid as a girl to bring her Chinese friends to her own home ? Surely it was because her heroic father, whose character she has movingly portrayed in *Fighting Angel*, would have been quite insensitive to the impropriety of seeking to evangelize such guests, unless he was truly prepared to be identified with them—up to and including the point of intermarriage. After all the ups and downs of her public and private life, it seems more than a coincidence that in the end Pearl Buck has found great happiness and satisfaction in working in the United States to alleviate the lot of unwanted children of mixed Chinese and American parentage.

At the end of the last century missionaries went and died physically with the utmost heroism in West Africa, the ' white man's grave '. West Africa is no longer the white man's grave in that original sense, but may it not well be that the missionary cause here depends today on our understanding that term in a deeper and more profound sense ? If it be argued that the cost of such total integration or identification is too high—and that the children of any mixed marriage, for example, have to suffer in ways for which no parents could rightly contemplate responsibility, surely the answer is that the real meaning of true crucifixion with Christ has always to do more with its effect upon others than upon ourselves. Jesus may have been thinking of himself in Gethsemane, but surely he was thinking much more of others, Mary, Mary Magdalene, Peter, James, John, all the disciples, the Jewish people and the Roman governor and, above all, perhaps the leaders of the Jewish church, when he cried, " Abba, Father, all things are possible unto thee ; remove this cup from me : howbeit not what I will, but what thou wilt ".[1]

If the missionary cause of Jesus Christ is to prevail, it can only be by the way of the true cross. There can be no Pentecostal Spirit without Calvary. The pietist Spirit can perhaps be given before the cross : the Pentecostal Spirit can certainly only be given after it. Perhaps nowhere has the present predicament and possibility of the missionary movement been more clearly stated than in the resolution of the Willingen Missionary Conference in 1952 : " The eternal gospel must be so presented to men and women that its contemporary and compelling

[1] Mark 14 : 36

relevance is recognized. It cannot be recognized as long as it appears in a foreign guise, imitating and reproducing the characteristics of a church in some remote and alien land. Foreign in one sense the Church must always be ; its citizenship is in heaven, and it is an agent of transformation. Despite the dangers of identification with this world, we urge that foreignness in the more earthly sense of the word is something to be outgrown with all possible speed." [1]

This is far easier said than done. For American missionaries to accept it with enthusiasm in theory at Meadville or at Seabury House is one thing : for them, or for any others, to accept its far-reaching implications in practice in Asia or Africa or Latin America is quite another. Yet how can any church unity, let alone world unity, be conceived except on some such basis ? For this surely is the heart of the purpose of God and the deepest secret of the way he works. If to save man he had to become man, how can we carry on his work if we refuse to follow his example ? There is a moving passage in Amy Wilson Carmichael's great spiritual legacy, *Gold Cord*, in which she pauses to reflect on the tragedy of many missionaries, who have given up so much for Christ and yet hold back the one thing needful. " To me," she quotes, " there is no more tragic sight than the average missionary. A Hindu bowing down to his idol leaves me unmoved beside it. We have given so much, yet not the one thing that counts ; we aspire so high, and fall so low ; we suffer so much, but so seldom with Christ ; we have done so much, and so little will remain ; we have known Christ in part, and have so effectively barricaded our hearts against His mighty love, which surely He must yearn to give His disciples above all people." [2]

It is impossible to exaggerate the agony with which

[1] cf. G. Appleton, *The Divine Strategy* (S.C.M., n.d.), p. 14
[2] Amy Carmichael, *Gold Cord* (S.P.C.K., 1932), p. 10

Peter and Paul faced the apparent betrayal of all that, racially, religiously and morally, their people had held sacred for a thousand years. No wonder it required both the example and inspiration of Calvary and also the direct guidance and inspiration of the Pentecostal Spirit to get them to follow Stephen's fearless lead and break down the barriers which separated Jews from Gentiles. The achievement of reunion in South India has been described as " a dangerous experiment " ; so in a sense was the incarnation, and so is almost every venture to which the Pentecostal Spirit would lead the church of those who have been truly baptized into Christ's death not only in the rite of a moment but also as a principle of a lifetime, and so are prepared to " go forth . . . without the camp, bearing his reproach ".[1]

[1] Hebrews 13 : 13

CHAPTER VII

THE FIRE OF UNITY AND THE PAULINE SPIRIT

PAUL, more than any other apostle, is responsible for the full Christian doctrine of the Holy Spirit. He did two things. First, he saw the Spirit's work in all kinds of human behaviour, gifts, talents, aptitudes, and skills within the Christian church. This prevented the local church from becoming a clique. Secondly, he, more than Peter or any other apostle, was a living example of the Pentecostal Spirit. He not only smashed " the middle wall of partition " between Jews and Gentiles but also insisted on a thorough-going application of the principle that there is " no distinction " [1] between them. " All have sinned " and all can be saved in the same way and on the same terms. This prevented the universal church from becoming a clique.

The reason why Paul was able to give such a wonderful comprehensiveness to the doctrine of the Spirit was because he had such a rich experience of the Spirit in his own life. During his pre-Christian boyhood and training he must have been influenced by both the pietist and the philosophical Spirit. In describing his early years he says, " from my youth up . . . after the straitest sect of our religion I lived a Pharisee ".[2] His religious environment, first at Tarsus and then at Jerusalem, cannot have been totally different from the pietism in which Jesus was brought up. And, in addition, he was educated by Gamaliel,[3] who was perhaps the most liberal and most philosophically minded of all the Jewish rabbis of the time.

[1] Romans 3 : 22   [2] Acts 26 : 4 f.
[3] Acts 22 : 3

Then came his dramatic conversion on the Damascus road. Of all the apostles, he had the most vivid and spectacular experience, and after such a volcanic explosion he could never deny the supreme importance of the breaking through of the primitive Spirit. This was not something which he afterwards outgrew. On the contrary, he could write to the Corinthians, who knew all about primitive ecstasy, and claim that he spoke with tongues more than any of them.[1] Indeed, he gives hints of all sorts of abnormal visions and experiences, which he is very reluctant to talk about.[2]

But there was more to his dramatic conversion than the work of the primitive Spirit. For he remained blind after his experience for three days until " a certain disciple at Damascus, named Ananias ",[3] came and laid his hands on him and baptized him. This was the work of the priestly Spirit, and in the same context of his conversion, Paul puts his call to the Gentile mission [4]—clear evidence of the presence of the prophetic Spirit. (The way in which so many different elements of the Spirit's work are combined in the same experience is clear proof of how artificial in life is the distinction in analysis between them).

It was the prophetic Spirit who opposed the temptation Paul must have felt to keep the Gentile Christians separate from the Jews and also to expect them to accept the Old Testament Jewish ideas of what was clean and what was unclean. The Epistle to the Galatians is a fiery blast of the same Spirit, directed against any insistence that Gentile Christians must be circumcised as well as baptized. There could be no question of compromise on the issue of segregation. Christian Jews must be prepared to eat as well as worship with Christian Gentiles. Paul saw this more clearly than Peter, even though as an unmarried man he may not have realized as clearly as

[1] 1 Corinthians 14 : 18   [2] 2 Corinthians 12 : 1 ff.
[3] Acts 9 : 10   [4] Acts 26 : 17

Peter the far-reaching implications for the family of complete social integration.[1]

Thus Paul recapitulated in his own life and experience all the stages of the Spirit's work, which we have outlined—primitive, prophetic, priestly, philosophical and pietist—and he was himself in his missionary activity the supreme apostolic exponent of the Pentecostal Spirit. His work is totally misconstrued if it is seen as merely itinerant evangelism. What itinerant evangelist, for example, would have gone on lecturing in the school of Tyrannus at Ephesus every day for two years, especially if it meant losing his siesta to do it ![2] He was not just preaching the gospel, he was creating a new community across the barriers and divisions of the ancient world. If he dreamed when he wrote to the Ephesians of the final summing up of everything in Christ,[3] he had spent quite a long time at Ephesus starting to do the sum himself.

It was his vision of the unity and inclusion of all things in the loving purpose of God that more and more filled his horizon, as his mind moved from the trembling expectation of an imminent 'second coming' in the Epistles to the Thessalonians towards the majestic sweep and cosmic scope of the divine plan, outlined in the Epistles to the Colossians and Ephesians. But though the scale of his canvas was transformed, the portrait he wished always to paint was the same. No new vistas of knowledge revealed by the philosophical Spirit ever shifted Paul one inch from the burning vision of the love of God revealed in Christ crucified, which was at the heart of his experience of the primitive Spirit on the Damascus road.

The voice that said to him, " I am Jesus whom thou persecutest ",[4] convinced him of two things. First, there could be no separation of the Spirit from Jesus, for it was Jesus who was at the heart of his own shattering spiritual

---

[1] Galatians 2 : 11 ff.   [2] So one manuscript of Acts 19 : 9
[3] Ephesians 1 : 10   [4] Acts 9 : 5

experience. Secondly, there could be no separation of Jesus from the church, for it was the Christian members of the " body " of Christ whom Paul had in fact been persecuting and on whose further persecution he was at that very moment bent.

It was the Spirit who thus first opened Paul's eyes to the wonder of Jesus Christ, and he found that the more he trusted the Spirit, the more his eyes were opened to that amazing wonder. And the more his eyes were so opened, the more he realized the unimaginable possibilities of life " in the Spirit ". In fact, he was living in the ' wonderland ' of love, not in sentimental imagination but in hard fact, and what it meant to him he put down in the unforgettable poem of 1 Corinthians 13. It was living ' in love ' in this sense that enabled him to realize what the Spirit was capable of doing for the church and for every member of it. The " fruit " [1] of the Spirit was the secret of a rich moral character, and the inward " witness " of the Spirit [2] was the secret of prayer and communion with God. It was the Spirit who empowered the Christian ministry [3] and enabled all kinds of things to happen that were otherwise inconceivable : " The word of wisdom . . . the word of knowledge . . . faith . . . gifts of healings . . . workings of miracles . . . prophecy . . . discerning of spirits . . . divers kinds of tongues . . . the interpretation of tongues . . . all these worketh the one and the same Spirit, dividing to each one severally even as he will." [4]

If we try to bring together the gifts and qualities of character which Paul attributes to the Spirit and group them according to our analysis of the evidence of the Spirit's work in the Bible, then under the heading of the primitive Spirit will perhaps come such things as tongues, healings and miracles, all of which are unmistakable and

[1] Galatians 5 : 22   [2] Romans 8 : 16, 26
[3] 1 Corinthians 12 : 28
[4] 1 Corinthians 12 : 8 ff. ; cf. 1 Corinthians 12 : 28 ff.

yet, in our present state of knowledge, to a greater or less degree rationally inexplicable. As for the prophetic Spirit, Paul would perhaps have included among his gifts not only prophecy, but also discerning of spirits, knowledge, faith, and perhaps the interpretation of tongues, though it is impossible to draw a hard and fast line between the prophetic and the philosophical Spirit.[1] Undoubtedly Paul knew as much of the philosophical Spirit as anyone in the early church, but though he puts wisdom among the gifts of the Spirit, the threat of Gnosticism made him careful to insist to the Colossians that it was " Christ, in whom are all the treasures of wisdom and knowledge hidden ".[2] And any tendency to overweight the gifts of the philosophical Spirit on the theoretical side is balanced by an equal insistence on his part in providing practical ' helps ' and ' governments ',[3] for the church.

The evidence for Paul's belief in and reliance upon the priestly Spirit is clearly seen in the central place which he assumed for the eucharist (to which he ascribed physical as well as spiritual benefits [4]) and in the fact that he not only baptized converts—sometimes very reluctantly [5]—but also (if that was not part and parcel of the same rite) " laid his hands upon them ". [6] " Apostles " head the list of those " set . . . in the church " [7] by God, and in the rite of ordination to the apostolic ministry there seems to have been a remarkable combination of both the prophetic and the priestly work of the Spirit. The evidence for this combination is clear in one of the accounts of Timothy's ordination,[8] and in what may well have been Paul's own ordination,[9] even though it is usually regarded merely as a valedictory service. This

[1] cf. Isaiah 11 : 2a
[2] Colossians 2 : 2 ff.
[3] 1 Corinthians 12 : 28
[4] 1 Corinthians 11 : 30
[5] 1 Corinthians 1 : 14 ff.
[6] e.g. cf. Acts 19 : 6
[7] 1 Corinthians 12 : 28
[8] 1 Timothy 4 : 14, but cf. 2 Timothy 1 : 6
[9] Acts 13 : 3

occurred at Antioch at the start of the first missionary journey. It was the prophetic Spirit who told the leaders of the local church whom to appoint as missionaries. And " when they had fasted and prayed and laid their hands on them, they sent them away ".[1]

The procedure is identical with Paul's description of Timothy's ordination.[2] This would seem conclusive evidence that what happened at Antioch was an ordination. Yet Paul says to the Galatians that he was an apostle " not from men, neither through man ".[3] He could not possibly have said this, if his apostleship dated only from his Antiochene ordination. The inference is clear : the " prophets and teachers ",[4] who were the leaders of the church at Antioch, ordained someone who was already an apostle, appointed by Jesus Christ himself—and there is no sign that the apostle thought this extraordinary or *infra dig*. There is thus a quite remarkable combination of prophetic and priestly elements at the heart not only of Paul's personal conversion experience but also of primitive ministerial church practice.

As for the pietist Spirit, that is the secret of the intimate communion which was at the heart of Paul's spiritual life. To be " in Christ " meant for him to be in the Spirit and thus to experience his inner guidance, witness and intercession [5] and also to bring forth the fruit of the Spirit—" love, joy, peace, long suffering, kindness, goodness, faithfulness, meekness, temperance ".[6] The spiritual " witness " and the ethical " fruit " combine in the hymn to love in 1 Corinthians 13, which is the crown and climax of the Pauline teaching about the gifts of the Spirit. If instead of the word ' love ' or ' charity ' in that chapter we read ' Jesus ', we have the most perfect description of Jesus' own life and character that an apostolic pen could give.

---

[1] Acts 13 : 3
[2] 1 Timothy 4 : 14
[3] Galatians 1 : 1
[4] Acts 13 : 1
[5] Romans 8 : 14 ff., 27
[6] Galatians 5 : 22 f.

It was into a community filled with the pietist Spirit that Jesus was born, and it was the work of the Pentecostal Spirit, of which Paul was the supreme exponent, to plant all over the eastern Mediterranean world little colonies of deep pietist devotion, in which it could perhaps truly be said that Jesus was again and again reborn. The life Paul wrote about in 1 Corinthians 13 he expected to be lived in Corinth—and by first generation converts at that ! But he expected the life he wrote about in 1 Corinthians 12 to be lived there, too. He was not prepared for a pietist clique of love any more than for a Pauline or a Petrine or even a Christian [1] clique to masquerade as the church of God.

In the end he was prepared to sacrifice everything, even the dreams of world-wide evangelization that were dearest to his heart, for the sake of church unity. That was why he insisted on taking the Gentile collection up to Jerusalem and why, when he got there, he was so scrupulous not to offend Jewish Christian susceptibilities [2] that he found himself involved in a temple riot and taken into protective custody by the Roman military authorities. It is hardly an exaggeration to say that he ended up a prisoner in Rome instead of an evangelist in Spain [3] precisely because, when it came to an issue, he put church unity before world evangelization. He realized that the latter could not succeed, unless the former was maintained.

*   *   *   *   *

" Workers of the world, unite ! " was the spark that in 1848 set alight a fire that has now consumed half the world. There is fire in every sincere call for unity ; it may be diabolical or it may be divine, but it cannot be ignored. We have only to think of the passions aroused by the call for Arab unity in the Middle East or by the

---

[1] 1 Corinthians 1 : 12   [2] cf. Acts 21 : 26 ff
[3] Romans 15 : 24, 28

Cypriot demand for *enosis*, or union, with Greece. But far deeper than the political hunger for unity is the spiritual hunger, which is born today both out of fear of what will happen without such unity and out of hope of what might happen as a result of it.

The true passion for unity knows that no general theory is of any value unless it can be worked out in particular detail, but that the particular detail must be worked out in relation to a general theory. Cardinal Mercier said that " in order to unite you must love ; in order to love, you must know ; in order to know, you must meet one another ". Paul's passion was for unity of this sort, to be achieved in this way. He was not a fanatic, seeking to create a clique of like-minded fiery enthusiasts ; he was an apostle, setting people all over the Eastern Mediterranean world on fire with love for God and their fellow men, and so creating the Christian church across all the divisions of race, culture and class. If we want to see signs of a similar fire of unity today, we must look for it not in any narrow clique, but in the widest possible context of those who " profess and call themselves Christians ".

The primitive Spirit can be seen among the Pentecostal sects and in the Salvation Army and the Revival Movement. The prophetic Spirit can be seen in Protestantism, and the priestly Spirit in Catholicism, but this broad distinction is very misleading and, in the light of Paul's experience and practice, we may well ask to what extent (if any) both elements are present in either Protestant or Catholic services of Christian initiation or ordination today. The philosophical Spirit lives among modern Quakers and in the strongly intellectual emphasis of the worship of Presbyterians and European Protestants. The pietist Spirit can be seen in many inter-denominational groups, among old-fashioned Quakers, and the Brethren, and in cells of devotion of one sort or another throughout Christendom. If we knew more of Eastern

Orthodoxy, we might find all these elements alive the other side of the iron curtain.

As for the Pentecostal Spirit, this has broken down many barriers between Christians in the last seventy-five years, but only one truly creative experiment in church unity across, or at least partially across, the great gulf between Catholics and Protestants has so far been successful. The Church of South India does not need to be romanticized, as if it is perfect. But at least it can offer a clearer pointer to the working of the Pentecostal Spirit than any other church in Christendom.

Only where we can see something of all these elements of the Spirit's work can we be sure that the Pauline Spirit is at work. Perhaps some small communities, which are not cliques, may show its working more clearly than larger groups or churches, because only at a deep personal level can true unity be found, and that deep personal level is more easily realized among a few friends than in large crowds. If the Œcumenical Institute at Bossey, near Geneva, had more of the primitive and priestly Spirit, it would be a splendid example. If the Rev. Norman Motley's experiment at Othona had more of the priestly and philosophical Spirit, it would be even better. Best of all, perhaps, is the Iona Community, provided it does not despise the pietist Spirit, so congenial to its geographical situation and historical associations.

In small groups like these there is a chance of so meeting other people and representatives of other churches that we get to know them, and of so knowing them that we get to love them (with all their faults) and of so loving them that we unite with them. There is no short cut to unity, as Paul knew better than anyone else. All the letters he wrote (with the possible exception of Ephesians) were written to individuals or small local churches. That was how the Pauline Spirit created and maintained unity. The grand sweep of his words must not blind us to the very restricted circle of the readers he had in mind.

Only in small groups do we, in fact, become enough like little children to feel so secure of God that we can trust him not to let us lose in conversation with others anything spiritually vital or significant in our experience or heritage.   Fear of such loss is bound to destroy in advance any chance of success in discussions about reunion, which have not taken the time and trouble to get this basis of personal friendship first established among those taking part.   Especially in the Western world today there is the certainty that, without such a basis of true friendship, the primitive Spirit will be inhibited in advance from being able to do anything, because of our ingrained fear of being despised, if we show any enthusiasm or let ourselves be carried away by any cause.

The true Christian coming together in unity will not involve any cheapening of those things in our spiritual heritage which we hold dear.   On the contrary, in the small group of friends we can learn to appreciate what others value as well as realize the value of our own treasures, which otherwise we so easily take for granted. A visit to the United States two years ago showed me how true this was.   I had the privilege of preaching in churches of many denominations and of attending the inter-denominational missionary conference at Meadville, Pennsylvania, as well as the Episcopalian missionary conference at Seabury House, Connecticut.   The experience opened my eyes to many aspects of the life of other churches in other parts of the world, of which I was ignorant, and made me realize how much I needed to learn from them.   It also made me value my own Anglican heritage far more than I had done before.

Even though the Christian church cannot be seen in its fulness in any one denomination today, there may be some value in taking one denomination and showing how far the Pauline Spirit is able to express itself through such a broken vessel.   The Church of England happens to be my own church and the church, therefore, that I know best. If it can serve as an example, it can at least by its often abused, and sometimes far too loudly vaunted, comprehensiveness, show the difference between a church and a clique. It is the variety of the signs of life within it at the present time which gives some ground for hope that here can be seen in some measure the " fire " of the Pauline Spirit " upon the earth ".

Let me give a few illustrations, starting from where I live in Cornwall. The Anglican nuns of the Convent of the Epiphany in Truro run a wonderful old people's home at St Agnes—a model of relations between the church and the welfare state—and have a daughter house of sisters in Tokyo, in Japan. Over the county border there is in Devonshire, near Newton Abbot, the community of the Good Shepherd, a sisterhood concentrating on the life of prayer ; and on the north coast near Lynton among majestic scenery the quite different virile and enterprising evangelistic centre of Lee Abbey. In the next county, Dorset, the community centred on Cerne Abbas has brought back the Franciscan spirit into Anglicanism, and I am proud to think that its founder was once curate of a well-known Evangelical church in Oxford with which I also have had some connection. If from Dorset we move to Hampshire, Canon Roger Lloyd of Winchester has been the guiding spirit behind the cell movement of the Servants of Christ the King, which is active in a pastoral and evangelistic work, springing from a deep spirit of prayer and devotion. Finally, from Hampshire we can move over the county border to Sussex and there find the community of St Julian's near Horsham in Sussex, founded by Miss Florence Allshorn, offering recuperation of body, mind and spirit to tired missionaries and others, looking after their children and running a farm.

To these few examples, selected solely because of their geographical position, must be added the Parish and People Movement, which has put back (without party bias) the family communion at the centre of church life in many parishes since the last war. Not all its work has been as spectacular as the success of Canon Mervyn Stockwood in Bristol, in creating a vital local fellowship with his Free Church brethren, or of Canon Ernest Southcott in Leeds in making a true church community out of a new housing area, or of Canon E. R. Wickham [1] in forging effective evangelistic links between the church and industry in Sheffield. But perhaps the most significant feature of life in the Church of England today is the unspectacular way in which in parish after parish, according to no stereotyped pattern, the family life of the church is reviving and in consequence effecting imperceptibly a transformation of its evangelistic witness.

This is a sign of the work of the Pauline Spirit, and it is not by any means the only sign. The past twenty-five years have seen a complete change in the relationship between Catholics and Evangelicals within the Church of England. Increasingly now the true Anglican is genuinely torn between the pull of Rome on the one hand and Geneva on the other. No longer are Catholics so convinced that all the truth is in Rome or Protestants that it is all in Geneva. Many Evangelicals have begun to realize that mediæval vestments, which are worn by good Swedish Lutherans, need not necessarily imply a doctrine which they cannot hold. Many Catholics, encouraged by Papal pronouncements, have begun to rediscover the point and purpose of having evening celebrations of holy communion and of " reading the Bible biblically ", as the Dominicans say.[2] And if the work of unity in life has still far to go, in literature the frontiers are wide open—there is a unity in theology which would have been unthinkable a generation ago—and in liturgy there is renewed hope that the attempt to revise *The*

---

[1] cf. E. R. Wickham, *Church and People in an Industrial City* (Lutterworth Press, 1957)

[2] B. Frost, *The Art of Mental Prayer* (Philip Allan, 1935), p. 13

Book of Common Prayer, which proved such a disastrous failure in 1927 and 1928, may prove to be a practical possibility in the near future.

All this is a typical example from one church of what the Pauline Spirit is doing all over Christendom today. There is not only a new breath of hope and a new dynamic of faith, but also a much more genuine awareness of past sins and present shortcomings. Every spiritual advance towards Christian unity has been marked by a new and deeper awareness of the need for contrition and true repentance. This is as true among Roman Catholics as among Protestants, as the following quotation from an American news magazine illustrates : " A little after midnight on the 24th of August, 1572, began the famed massacre of St Bartholomew's Day, in which some 2000 Huguenots were killed by the mob in Paris alone. Last week, in hundreds of Roman Catholic churches throughout France, special Masses were said to ask forgiveness for this crime against fellow Christians, and many Protestant ministers also took note of the occasion to ask their congregations to forgive and forget. This observance of St Bartholomew's Day has grown year by year since 1937, when it was started by Abbé Paul Coutourier, an ex-school teacher who had found his vocation as priest at the age of 56. Until his death in 1953, grey, scholarly Abbé Coutourier devoted himself to encouraging understanding and co-operation among churches. He once succeeded in persuading a Catholic missionary magazine to devote an entire issue to the work of Protestant missions." [1]

An Episcopalian comment [2] on this calls for Christian penitence all round, and if the Pauline Spirit is working amongst us today, there will be much more genuine penitence. But there will also be much more genuine faith, expressing itself in courageous and widely different activities in and through the universal church. Perhaps

[1] *Time*, September 2nd, 1957, p. 34   [2] *Time*, loc. cit.

it is not without significance that the Roman Catholic and Anglican emphasis on repentance is in the same issue of *Time* immediately preceded by an account of the Third Assembly of the Lutheran World Federation at Minneapolis, which ends with this quotation from Dr Franklin Clark Fry. " At Lund, Sweden, in 1947, Lutherans learned to march together," he said. " At Hanover, Germany, in 1952, they learned to pray together. At Minneapolis in 1957, they learned to think together." On this, perhaps the comment of the Pauline Spirit might well be, " All things are yours ; whether Paul, or Apollos, or Cephas " (dare we substitute " Geneva or Wittenberg or Epworth or Canterbury or Rome " ?) " or the world, or life, or death, or things present, or things to come ; all are yours ; and ye are Christ's ; and Christ is God's ".[1]

If we are a long way from this at present, at least we know the way forward. Unity depends on love, love on knowledge, and knowledge on meeting one another. We cannot improve upon Cardinal Mercier's " golden sequence ". This does not mean that we despise inter-denominational conferences or inter-church discussions, but it means that we realize that nothing they can do to bring us closer together will be of any use unless at the same time we meet personally and so get to know and love one another. Only in such an atmosphere of personal friendship shall we be able to see which of our hitherto imagined principles are in fact ingrained prejudices, and what parts of the supposedly heretical outlook of others must be taken into our own system, if we are to be fully orthodox. It is one thing to pray to God :

> *The dearest idol I have known,*
> *Whate'er that idol be,*
> *Help me to tear it from Thy throne*
> *And worship only Thee.*

[1] 1 Corinthians 3 : 21–23

It is quite another thing to let the Pauline Spirit open
our eyes to our idolatry through the words of a Roman
Catholic priest, a Presbyterian elder, a Methodist minister
or a Plymouth Brother.   But how else is he likely to be
able to do it ?

CHAPTER VIII

THE FIRE OF LOVE AND THE PARACLETE

THE wonder of the Pauline doctrine of the Spirit is its inclusive and comprehensive character, by which the most diverse aspects of Christian discipleship and the most dissimilar characteristics of individual temperament and corporate community life are held together in a unity ; but that very wonder carries with it a corresponding peril. How can we be sure that the Spirit who is expressed in such radically different ways is the same as the Spirit of Jesus Christ ? This is a real problem, and it is accentuated rather than diminished by Paul's own shattering assertion : " Even though we have known Christ after the flesh, yet now we know him so no more." [1] Put such a remark into the context of a first century Gentile community, take away from that community any surviving personal links with and reminiscences at first or second hand of Jesus himself, set that community in the midst of all sorts of wild Gnostic speculations on the relationship between God and the world, and you begin to get some idea of the kind of problem that caused S. John to write his interpretation of Christianity in the form not of a series of letters or of a doctrinal thesis but of a gospel—after the pattern of the Synoptists and yet entirely different from them.

The doctrine of the Paraclete,[2] in its awe-inspiring context of Jesus' last words to his disciples,[3] seems expressly designed to prevent the church being led astray down all the slippery slopes of Gnostic theological

[1] 2 Corinthians 5 : 16
[2] Paraclete is a transliteration of the Greek word, which can be translated " Advocate " or " Comforter " (=strengthener).
[3] cf. John 14 : 16, 26 ; 15 : 26 ; 16 : 7

speculation and erotic moral perversion. S. John tackles the problem of spiritual activity unrelated to Jesus Christ by emphasizing that the Spirit himself, where he is truly understood as Holy, invariably points to Jesus Christ. The tie-up is complete : Jesus and the Holy Spirit cannot be separated. This does not deny the lower ranges of the Spirit's more ostentatious phenomena ; it does not despise either primitive abnormalities or Pentecostal exuberance ; it underlines the Pauline principle of unity, embracing all the rich variety of spiritual experiences, and it identifies that principle with Jesus himself. Here, in Jesus' last discourses, is the heart of the doctrine of the Holy Spirit of self-effacing love. These few references are the standard by which ultimately all the Spirit's manifestations can be measured.

But they must be understood in their proper Johannine context. At the outset of the Fourth Gospel John the Baptist bears witness to the descent of the Spirit upon Jesus at his baptism.[1] Nicodemus is told of the paramount necessity for a re-birth " of water and the Spirit ".[2] If this is either sheer lunacy or an incomprehensible miracle to a great theologian, it is nevertheless an indisputable reality in the life of a simple believer. To the woman of Samaria the fundamental emphasis is not so much on re-birth (she probably recognized the need for this much more readily than Nicodemus) as on the necessity for all true worship of God as Spirit and as Father to be " in spirit and truth ".[3] To these positive affirmations must be added the corrective to any carnally materialistic doctrine of the eucharist, provided by the categorical assertion that " It is the spirit that quickeneth; the flesh profiteth nothing ".[4]

Yet all these Johannine references to the Spirit in the life of Jesus cannot obscure the fact (of which S. John was well aware) that, as a distinct and recognizably different

[1] John 1 : 32 ff.   [2] John 3 : 5
[3] John 4 : 23 f.   [4] John 6 : 63

mode of divine activity, the Spirit was a post-crucifixion phenomenon in the Christian church. S. John may cut down the Synoptic interval between Good Friday and Whitsunday to two days but, whether on Easter Day on a few [1] or on the Day of Pentecost on many, what matters is that the Spirit then came in a way he had not done before. In either case there was a reality of God's presence and power in the Christian church after Calvary which was not previously available for others besides Jesus himself.

It was to explain the nature and work of this post-crucifixion reality that Jesus himself expounded in the last Johannine discourses the doctrine of the Paraclete. It is the Paraclete who alone is an adequate substitute for Jesus, and by his presence in the church—not in the world—he will not so much make up for the physical absence of Jesus as achieve his perpetual spiritual presence.[2]

This makes possible, after the crucifixion and resurrection, missionary achievements through the church out of all proportion to Jesus' own achievements in his earthly ministry. These are the " greater works " [3] which he could not do in that ministry, but which his Spirit, liberated through his physical departure to work in hitherto undreamt-of ways, is able to do in and through the Christian church. It is the Spirit's work to convict not the church, but the world (but the world usually through the church) " in respect of sin, and of righteousness, and of judgement ".[4] This conviction is achieved not by any independent work of the Holy Spirit, acting on his own, but by his illumination of the meaning and significance of Jesus and his crucifixion. By showing (usually through the church) what this means to those outside the church, he makes possible all the church's successful evangelistic and missionary enterprises. In the

---

[1] John 20 : 22   [2] John 14 : 16 ff.
[3] John 14 : 12   [4] John 16 : 8

Johannine Paraclete is to be found no improvement upon Jesus himself, but the source of all the true glorification of Jesus which has gone on finding expression in the Christian church from the first century up till today.[1]

To see how this high doctrine of the Paraclete works out in humble practice, we can best turn to the Synoptic evidence about Jesus himself. This evidence may sometimes represent a reading back into Jesus' life and ministry of interpretations of God's activity in terms of the Holy Spirit, which are more likely to be part of the church's vocabulary than her Lord's. But if so, that only shows in what kind of situation the early church proved the power of the Holy Spirit. The evidence begins with Jesus' baptism. It is the unanimous testimony of all four Gospels [2] that the immediate sequel to Jesus' baptism by John was the descent of the Spirit upon him. He was not baptized in order to get the Spirit (that would be only a refined version of the sin of simony [3]), but after he was baptized, the Spirit was given. And the early church knew that what was true for the Master in his unique vocation was true also for his disciples in their humbler vocations. If his baptism preceded the gift of the Spirit, so did theirs. If his baptism was followed by the gift of the Spirit, they could expect the same to be true of theirs. If exceptions to this order occurred—and they did—then they might cause some surprise but certainly no dismay. They merely proved the general rule that baptism into Christ's death was the prelude to the gift of his Holy Spirit. This did not mean that the outward water rite of a moment was any substitute for the inward spiritual principle of a lifetime. On the contrary, it was precisely as an initiation into that inward principle that it released and made available hitherto undreamt-of energies of the Holy Spirit.

[1] John 16 : 13 ff.
[2] Mark 1 : 9–11 ; Matthew 3 : 13–17 ; Luke 3 : 21 f. ; John 1 : 32 f.
[3] Acts 8 : 18 f.

If these energies begin to be released through Christian initiation, they go on finding expression throughout the Christian life, and especially in times of temptation and persecution. The Synoptic Gospels go so far as to say that the circumstances of Jesus' temptation, if not the temptation itself, were engineered by the Holy Spirit.[1] It was in the fierce fires of such inner struggles that, as the early church well knew, the power of the " Advocate " more than balanced the power of " the accuser ".[2] And these inner struggles were of a piece with the great agonies of outer persecution, in which Jesus' guarantee of the help of the Holy Spirit was vindicated over and over again in the experience of the martyrs.[3]

The early Christians expected the same extra help from the Holy Spirit when they undertook their missionary and evangelistic enterprises. The text [4] of Jesus' ' inaugural '—his Nazareth sermon—must have led them to expect a similar enduement of spiritual power when they got up to speak. Confession of Christ seems in the early church often to have been accompanied by evidence of the Holy Spirit,[5] and such confession could be made equally well in personal conversation, public evangelistic preaching, and *extempore* or liturgical prayers. But it is significant that it was in an evangelistic and missionary context—the great mission charge—that the promise of the Holy Spirit to help in speaking was originally given.[6]

If then the Spirit was pre-eminently connected with Christian initiation and Christian missionary activity and preaching, especially when faced by persecution, he was certainly the hall-mark of Christian communion [7] and worship. This is not at all to make conscious

---

[1] Mark 1 : 12 f. ; Matthew 4 : 1 ff. ; Luke 4 : 1 ff.
[2] Revelation 12 : 10
[3] Mark 13 : 11 ; Matthew 10 : 17 ff. ; Luke 12 : 11 f.
[4] Luke 4 : 18 f.   [5] 1 John 4 : 1 ff.
[6] Matthew 10 : 19 ff.   [7] 2 Corinthians 13 : 14

experience the yard-stick by which members of the Christian community should measure their spiritual standing : the first beatitude is a salutary corrective against any such forms of glib self-delusion.[1] But the presence of the Holy Spirit was the recognizable criterion of difference from the rest of the world by which the early Christians were thrilled again and again when they met to worship " in the Spirit on the Lord's day ".[2] It was this that drew them like a magnet to worship God every week at the peril of their lives before dawn on a working day. There was something different about such worship—and they called it the Spirit. It was as elusive and indefinable and as impossible to manufacture as the ' atmosphere ' of some churches, but it was an intense and undeniable reality, and more like some one than some thing. Therefore, blasphemy against the Holy Spirit was intolerable : to deny this reality or to ascribe it to a demonic rather than a divine source was to commit the unforgivable sin. For anyone to bring such a charge against Jesus, or for outsiders to bring such a charge against the church, or for one section of the church to bring that sort of charge against another section—that attitude, if persisted in, was spiritually suicidal.[3]

One clear conclusion can be drawn from the biblical evidence. Calvary precedes Pentecost : this is a psychological necessity as well as an historical fact. To seek for the Spirit is one thing, and such a search has Synoptic sanction in the Lukan version of Jesus' rhetorical question, " If ye then, being evil, know how to give good gifts unto your children, how much more shall your heavenly Father give the Holy Spirit to them that ask him ? "[4] But not to dodge the cross is another and a far more important thing : for it is on the cross of duty and discipline in our own life that the Holy Spirit of love is seeking us. Here and here only can we be " crucified

[1] Matthew 5 : 3   [2] Revelation 1 : 10
[3] Matthew 12 : 32 ; Luke 12 : 10   [4] Luke 11 : 13

with Christ ",[1] and baptism into Christ's death as the abiding principle of a lifetime as well as the critical rite of a moment, with all that that means in terms of its practical implications (in the crucifixion of self and identification with Christ's body, the church), is the fundamental condition of the filling of the Holy Spirit.

* * * * *

> *Come, Holy Ghost, our souls inspire,*
> *And lighten with celestial fire ;*
> *Thou the anointing Spirit art,*
> *Who dost thy sevenfold gifts impart ;*
>
> *Thy blessèd unction from above*
> *Is comfort, life, and fire of love ;*

These are the opening words of the only hymn in *The Book of Common Prayer*, and they come very near to the heart of the Johannine doctrine of the Paraclete. Here is " the fire of love ", and when we seek for signs of it " upon the earth ", two remarkable illustrations may help us in our search.

On November 23rd, 1654, from 10.30 p.m. to 12.30 a.m. at Paris, Blaise Pascal had an overwhelming experience. He could only describe it by one word, " Fire ". When he tried to explain what it meant, all he could say was, " God of Abraham, God of Isaac, God of Jacob, not of the philosophers and scientists . . . God of Jesus Christ. . . . He can be found only in the ways taught in the Gospel ".[2] Nearly four hundred years before, on December 6th, 1273, in the early morning at Naples Thomas Aquinas had an equally shattering experience, as a result of which he never wrote another word. " I can write no more," he told his companion, " for everything that I have written seems like straw by comparison

[1] Galatians 2 : 20
[2] cf. J. Chevalier, *Pascal* (Sheed and Ward, 1930), pp. 94 f.

with the things, which I have now *seen*, and which have been *revealed* to me." [1]

This is the fire of love, in which the Paraclete does not speak about himself, but on the contrary so effaces himself as to make all speech about him impossible and all talk on subjects other than Jesus Christ a waste of time. Where can we see such " fire upon the earth " today ? It will certainly not be advertised, but it may break out where the sacraments bring us back, from all our intellectual speculations and talk about spiritual experiences, to true baptismal identification and holy communion with Jesus Christ, and where the scriptures bring us back from all the wonders of the contemporary world and the examples of the saints of all ages to meditation upon Jesus Christ. Where this happens, and where both sacraments and scriptures are kept in their right place and are not allowed to usurp the position of the Holy Spirit within the Godhead, there the purest flame of the divine love has a chance to break forth " upon the earth ".

It is the aim and object both of the sacraments of the gospel and also of the written Gospels to keep Christ at the centre of the life and work and worship of the church. They prevent our getting away from him into the more rarified, but far less human, atmosphere of spirit- or saint-possession with all its dangers of eccentricity and pathological abnormality, if not of rank immorality. The Spirit must be given liberty of free expression. Acts shows what this means, and S. John gives us its warrant : " The Spirit breatheth where it listeth, and thou hearest the voice thereof, but knowest not whence it cometh and whither it goeth : so is every one that is born of the Spirit." [2] But to correct the apparently quite unpredictable outbursts of the Spirit, thus freely sanctioned and generously encouraged, running into unethical,

[1] cf. V. White, *God and the Unconscious* (Harvill Press, 1952), p. 139
[2] John 3 : 8 (margin)

unspiritual and anti-Christian channels, they must be closely related to Jesus Christ. To insist on this relationship is a major objective both of the Johannine doctrine of the Paraclete and of the church's sacramental system and canon of scripture.

But we must observe the biblical priorities : the Spirit is primary, the sacraments and scriptures are secondary ; the Spirit is in the Godhead, the sacraments and scriptures are not. The means of grace are not ends : they are indispensable aids to, but no substitutes for, that deeper knowledge of the Spirit and consequent ever-fresh reformulation of doctrine about him, which depend upon our, first, living in the true ' wonderland ' of love and, then, trying to describe it. It would be presumptuous to attempt to identify this self-effacing " fire " of love " upon the earth " today, but it may help to indicate three possible signs of its presence.

The first sign is likely to be true reconciliation to the way of the cross, as this has been revealed in the life and death of Jesus Christ. This means having the mind of Christ and therefore adopting naturally a Christ-like attitude to others. This will show itself not in looking down on them, but in looking up to them—not in any sentimental way, but with a soberly realistic appreciation of their sins and shortcomings. " Let this mind be in you, which was also in Christ Jesus : who . . . humbled himself." [1] Where we see Anglicans looking up to their Free Church and Roman Catholic brethren ; Christians looking up to Jews, Moslems and Buddhists ; Britons looking up to Germans, Egyptians and Italians ; High Church Catholics looking up to Low Church Protestants ; independent schools looking up to state schools ; white people looking up to black ; those who are not fundamentalists looking up to those who are—and all this *vice versa*, too—there we may see the fire of love.

Nowhere is this fire more apparent than among those

[1] Philippians 2 : 5 ff. A.V.

who share the mind of Christ on sin. Where we accuse someone of both religious fanaticism [1] and worldliness,[2] and find he or she is guilty of neither charge, there we may have stumbled unexpectedly across the clearest evidence of the Holy Spirit. Where we find someone completely identified with sinners (in reality—and not merely in benevolent or patronizing condescension), neither condemning them nor condoning their sin,[3] there we may have caught a far-off glimpse of " the Lamb of God, which taketh away the sin of the world ".[4]

The second sign of the fire of love may well be the resolute shouldering of responsibilities put in our path by God rather than the shouldering of other responsibilities of our own choosing in a perhaps quite unconscious attempt to dodge those that God has put in our path. No wonder the All-Africa Church Conference at Ibadan, Nigeria, in January 1958 was dubious about the eight-and-a-half million-dollar programme by which the Dutch Reformed Church hopes to provide suitable literature for non-white South Africans ! [5] But who of us can throw stones here ? Attempts to impress the world with our answer to what we think it needs are no substitute for attempts to express to the world the true answer to what it knows it needs. The modern parallel to the ' wandering scholars ' of the Middle Ages, seeking all over Europe the new learning of the Renaissance, may well be the continual stream of Africans coming to Great Britain to seek the new learning today. In a broadcast talk on April 22nd, 1958, Margaret Wigfield spoke of the pleasure of offering hospitality to such foreigners in her own home with her own family. But how much easier most of us find it to support missions overseas than to entertain foreigners at home !

[1] cf. Mark 3 : 21   [2] cf. Matthew 11 : 19
[3] cf. John 8 : 11   [4] John 1 : 29
[5] cf. The Christian Century (Chicago, Feb. 12, 1958), Vol. lxxv., No. 7, p. 191

The third sign of the fire of the Paraclete may be the most important of all—the redemption of charity from its debased significance of a dole to its true meaning of mutual and reciprocal love. The credal formula that the Holy Spirit proceeds " from the Father and the Son " is confirmation within the Godhead itself of a fundamental truth expressed in the incarnation, atonement and eucharist. God not only gives, he also takes ; and we are meant to " do..likewise ",[1] and not try to improve upon his example. The reciprocity of love is not the only fundamental truth enshrined within the Christian doctrine of the Godhead, but it is a very important truth, exceedingly relevant to our contemporary situation. The resolute attempt to carry out its implications would stop us doing to others what we should not like them to do to us.[2] It would make us abandon the one-way traffic street of charity as a dole, whether administered by Christians to non-Christians, as if we had all the truth and they none, or by one church or nation to another, or by whites to blacks, west to east, parents to children. It would make us come off our relatively safe, even if heroic, self-chosen and self-appointed one-way street on to the much more dangerous, even if humdrum, two-way traffic street of God's appointment and choice for us.[3]

A thorough-going application of the principle of reciprocity would do much more than reorientate missionary evangelism : it would transform preaching ; instead of being an oratorical display it would become a genuine conversation, " the organized Hallelujah of an

[1] Luke 10 : 37
[2] E.g. sending European missionaries to Africa when (in principle—regardless of whether it is a practical possibility) we are not prepared to receive African missionaries as our resident ministers over here.
[3] " England has saved herself by her exertions and Europe by her example " were Pitt's magnificent words in 1805. Suppose God wants to save us now by the exertions and example of others, are we willing for such salvation ?

ordered community."[1] It would transform prayer and worship : we should re-discover what the prayer *meeting* and the holy *communion* meant. It would give the Holy Spirit a chance to work, which otherwise he will never get—and what a transformation of our inter-denominational, inter-national, inter-racial and inter-religious scene would inevitably result !

If it be argued that we cannot do this for fear we may lose our own convictions, then the answer is clear. This is precisely the way to talk " with authority "[2] rather than merely from authorities. We are always prepared to enter into a genuine two-way conversation about things of which we are really sure. And, anyhow, if we cannot trust the Holy Spirit in such a context to look after all that is good and beautiful and true in what we hold dear, what can we trust him to do ? If it be argued that to go on this two-way traffic street would be to betray the strategy and policy of so many of our past saints and heroes, and especially those in the evangelistic and missionary tradition, then the answer is equally clear. By all means let us honour the saints and respect their tradition, but let them point to Christ, and not replace him ! As substitutes for him they are fatal obstacles to any reproduction in us of that true originality through which the Holy Spirit seeks to make Jesus Christ the contemporary of every age. He wants no copies—even of Jesus : he wants originals. The saints as means of grace are invaluable : as ends they are fatal, for as such they kill that creativity which is the birthright of all who are made in the image of the Creator.

For the one-way traffic street of giving we can find (or so it seems) many precedents from the heroes of present and past missionary and evangelistic endeavour, right back to Paul himself. But let them point us beyond

[1] P. T. Forsyth, *Positive Preaching and Modern Mind* (Hodder and Stoughton, 1897), p. 95
[2] Mark 1 : 27

themselves to Jesus, and there we shall find no one-way traffic street at all, but at every turn, from the moment he received flesh from Mary to the moment he received Simon's help in carrying his cross and Joseph of Arimathea's sepulchre in the garden, a reciprocal relationship of genuine give and take. This is the way he redeemed charity to its true significance, and we shall do well not to seek to improve upon his example, which in this as in many other ways was so much more human than many of the saints, and in consequence so infinitely more divine.

INDEX

A

Acts, 2, 4 ff., 15, 27, 33, 54, 73 ff., 86 ff., 104
Africa Inland Mission, 72
Africa, South, 7, 23, 32, 110
Agnes, St, 96
Ahab, 16 f.
Ahijah, 16 f.
Alabama, 23
Aldersgate Street, 69
Alexandria, 53
Allshorn, F., 96
Amos, 15, 21 f., 35
Ananias, 75, 87
Anathoth, 36
Andrews, C. F., 71
Anglicanism (cf. Church of England), 41, 95 ff., 109
Anna, 66
Annunciation, 64
Antioch, 91
Apartheid, 7, 26
Apollos, 99
Appleton, G., *quoted*, 84
Aquinas, 61, 107
Arab, 32, 92
Arimathea, Joseph of, 113
Aristotle, 61
Arkansas, 7
Ashram, 71
Assyria, 19, 21
Astarte, 3
Atonement, Day of, 37, 52
Attlee, C., 30
Augustine, 59, 61
Aztecs, 8

B

Baal, 3 ff., 7, 12
Babylon, 19
Baptism, x, 5, 9, 10, 11, 43, 85, 90, 102, 104, 107 f.
Barnabas, 75
Barrett, C. K., *quoted*, 74
Barth, K., 23, 59 f.
Bartholomew's Day, St, 98
Bathsheba, 17

Beaumont, G., 13, 47
Benedictus, 65
Benin, 8
Bethel, 22
Bezalel, 37
Bhave, V., 23
Bonhoffer, D. von, 23
Book of Common Prayer, The, 97 f., 107
Bossey, 94
Bradwell-on-Sea, 71
Brethren (see Plymouth Brethren)
Bristol, 97
Britain (British Commonwealth), 32
Brunner, E., 58
Buber, M., 16, 31
Buck, P., 82 f.
Buddhism, 61, 109
Bultmann, R., 60
Burma, 61

C

Cairo, 12, 48
Canterbury, 99
Carmichael, A., vii, viii, 71, 84
Cedd, St, 71
Cerne Abbas, 96
China Inland Mission, 72, 82
Christmas, 43, 56
Christian Century, The, 110
Chronicles, 2, 37
Chula, Prince, 61
Churchill, W., 30
Cincinnati, 33
Cluny, 13
Colossians, 53, 77, 88, 90
Commandments, Ten, 36
Communism, 7 ff., 24, 32
Confirmation, 9
Conversion, 87 f.
Corinthians, 1, vi, 8, 19, 87 ff., 99
Corinthians, 2, 38, 87, 101, 105
Cornelius, 75, 78
Cornwall, 44, 96
Coutourier, P., 98
Creation, 40, 63
Cripps, S., 31
Crusaders, 70, 72